MW00882162

I

WIN.

Faith Ain't Fair.

It's a Fight.

By Alissa Holt

Copyright © 2024 by Alissa Holt

I Win.

Faith Ain't Fair. It's a Fight.

by Alissa Holt

Printed in the United States of America.

Cover Design, Edited and Formatted by CSC Professional Editing & Creative Writing Services

Published by CSC Professional Editing & Creative Writing Services

All rights reserved solely by the author. The author guarantees all contents are original and do not infringe upon the legal rights of any other person or work. No part of this book may be reproduced in any form without the permission of the author. The views expressed in this book are not necessarily those of the publisher.

Scriptures marked NLT are taken from the HOLY BIBLE, NEW LIVING TRANSLATION (NLT): Scriptures taken from the HOLY BIBLE, NEW LIVING TRANSLATION, Copyright© 1996, 2004, 2007 by Tyndale House Foundation. Used by permission of Tyndale House Publishers, Inc., Carol Stream, Illinois 60188. All rights reserved. Used by permission.

Scriptures marked AMP are taken from the AMPLIFIED BIBLE (AMP): Scripture taken from the AMPLIFIED® BIBLE, Copyright © 1954, 1958, 1962, 1964, 1965, 1987 by the Lockman Foundation Used by Permission. (www.Lockman.org)

Scriptures marked KJV are taken from the KING JAMES VERSION (KJV): KING JAMES VERSION, public domain.

Scriptures marked NIV are taken from the NEW INTERNATIONAL VERSION (NIV): Scripture taken from THE HOLY BIBLE, NEW INTERNATIONAL VERSION ®. Copyright© 1973, 1978, 1984, 2011 by Biblica, Inc.™. Used by permission of Zondervan

Scriptures marked NKJV are taken from the NEW KING JAMES VERSION (NKJV): Scripture taken from the NEW KING JAMES VERSION®. Copyright© 1982 by Thomas Nelson, Inc. Used by permission. All rights reserved.

Scripture quotations marked TPT are from The Passion Translation®. Copyright © 2017, 2018, 2020 by Passion & Fire Ministries, Inc. Used by permission. All rights reserved. ThePassionTranslation.com.

Dedication

To the love of my life, Brandon Holt: Words aren't rich enough to carry the depth of our love. This one is the hardest to sign, with all the love letters left undone. Your name became my home, and your voice became sunlight on my darkest days. The rhythm of your heart became the song I'd forever sing, and the poem you recited washes over me with sweet memories:

I love you without knowing how or when, or from where.
I love you straightforwardly, without complexities or pride: so I love you because I know no other way other than this: where I does not exist, nor you.
So close that your hand on my chest is my hand. So close that your eyes close as I fall asleep.

-Pablo Neruda

To infinity and beyond, we loved, we fought, and we won.

-Liss

Table of Contents

Preface

Hey Friend,

If you're reading this, I assume you're navigating a less-than-perfect season. First, I want to say I'm sorry you're here. I wish I could meet you with coffee, comfort food and a space to cry it out. The best I can do is offer words on a page while praying this black-and-white space penetrates your soul in a way that brings faith to the surface.

This leads me to my second point: congratulations on your faith journey! Picking up this read and taking the steps to fight for your life is not an easy decision to make. I'm not claiming I'm an expert on the matter, but I can say, like most of us, I've had my fair share of trauma.

Nearly three years ago, I began writing the very book you're holding in your hands. I had just beat breast cancer for the first time, and if you had told me what was coming next, I may have shredded the entire thing. I had no idea winning faith would require a second round with the pink monster, fewer body parts and a deceased husband only four months after my double mastectomy. Still, I shared vulnerable moments throughout my journey by gaining an online following through social media and YouTube. Here, faith became active steps others watched rather than the aftermath of a story told.

Before you disconnect from this letter, let me be clear. I may be a breast cancer warrior and newly widowed, but this book is not a cancer guide or a documented pity party. It's a vulnerable guide to faith! Every one of our stories is laced with different realities and truths. Our struggles, circumstances and support system may differ significantly, but the answer remains the same: His name is Jesus.

The hard truth written within these pages is simple. Faith ain't fair; it's a fight. I know that's not necessarily easy to hear, especially when we didn't deserve the fight we've endured. Trust me, I know the struggle of that. But the reality is this:

God is good, and the devil is bad. It's true; the enemy is out to steal, kill and destroy everything God ordained for your life. My question is, how are you going to retaliate?

It wasn't until I began fighting for my life that I realized the direct correlation found in the fight of faith. You could apply everything I practiced to every single area of your faith walk, and I want to help you map it out. Here's what I've discovered. Are you ready? The Word of God truly equips us with everything necessary for a winning life. The problem is that we are often gifted with scripture and given zero steps to make it happen. When I wrote this book, my goal was not to share with you glazed-over religion concerning our faith walk. It was to empower you to lead yourself into a winning posture that takes back everything the Word says is yours. If God said it, I believe it, and that settles it!

Here's how it works: every chapter will begin with an unedited journal entry from my fight with the pink beast. From there, we'll dissect eight challenging areas by uncovering what it looks like to activate your faith. Throughout the chapters, you will notice three areas in bold print.

1. Write it.

2. Steps Towards Winning.

3. Pray it.

This is where I teach you how to apply the tools you are given. I provide challenges, journal prompts, exercises, targeted prayers and thought-provoking questions. See, I told you, this is not about throwing scripture your way; it's about pairing it with the steps to walk your faith out in a winning manner.

I want to give you permission to highlight in this book, fold pages and scribble tons of notes in the margins. Take time to truly dive into the depths of your faith journey by learning how to show up and fight authentically. I can't promise this will be easy, and I won't even say it'll turn out how you hope. I will say this: no one ever won a thing without first taking ownership. So many times, we desire others to fight for us, but at what point do we learn to lace up our own bootstraps?

This will be a journey, but let me throw a spoiler your way- you win!

I believe in you, God believes in you, but will you fight for you?

With all my love for coffee,

-Alissa

Chapter 1
Take Control

Journal

10/17/2020

So now wrap your heart tightly around the hope that lives within us. Knowing that God always keeps his promises.

- Hebrews 10:23, TPT

Hello,

The pages of this journal are currently empty, and I can't help but wonder how the stories written will play out. Although I haven't a clue what the details are, the truth is that God has already written, read and signed the book. I chose a journal covered in different flowers to represent the beauty, growth and life I'm determined to find in this season. They all have a different shade of pink, as I'm holding onto the promise that breast cancer can come with all *shades* from day to day.

There will be some that are deep and others that are light. I'll have moments that are rich and others that are sweet. There will be milestones that are big and others that are small. Regardless, they'll all be beautiful because they'll have promise within them.

Breast cancer is not a thing I ever thought I'd write about in a journal. I've written about depression, divorce, infertility and the pain of life, but never did I imagine this. Still, this is where I am, and you know what? It didn't take God by surprise. I'd be lying if I said I wasn't scared, but I'm not uncertain about the outcome. I will overcome because He has already overcome.

The promise I heard months before a diagnosis was made, still rings in my ears:

This will not be unto death, but it will be for My glory!

I'm holding onto it for dear life. I'm not done yet. I'm only getting started! Why would God bring me this far to let me die? I must believe He is a good Father, and His name is more significant than this disease.

Today, I received a text from my friend, Lisa. "I had a dream about you last night. I went to your house to ask something, and you were turned with your back facing me. I started to talk to you, and you turned and looked at me. Your face had a black covering on it, and it looked like it was shedding off and peeling. I told you that I missed you and I loved you. You hugged me tight and said, 'I'm not used to being frail.' I said, 'It's okay to be weak. We all have been there at some point in our lives.' You just kept crying on my shoulder. Then I saw you with a book, another book of your own. I told you your name would be big, and I saw you with a book deal. The book cover was pink, and you were on the front! Then, my dream was over. I love you!"

Lisa has no idea about the diagnosis that I've received. I've told no one except for family and the staff at our church. God keeps sending little reminders that He's in control. When I shared the news with the people we work with, our good friend, Jason, spoke up with tears streaming down his face. "You know what's crazy? I had a dream about you just last night! You and I were leaving the church together and were walking home. *[Both of our families live in parsonages on the church property.]* When we rounded the corner of the church, a man jumped out and attacked you. He stabbed you in your chest, and you began to wrestle him to the ground. I kept yelling to stop, but you wouldn't quit fighting this man. Eventually, he got up and took off. I immediately said, "We need to get an ambulance! You need help!" but you got up off the ground, bleeding and wounded, and kept walking. I told you to stop and that you must be treated, but you kept saying, "I have work to do! I don't have time for this! Too many people need me!"

Today, I trust that the process leads to promise because I have work to do, and too many people need my story. God cannot fail me.

-*Alissa*

The breath in my lungs weighed heavier than usual as I paced back and forth in front of the photo wall in our living room. My eyes darted from one picture to the next as I recalled the seasons of our lives. They captured free-spirited moments in open fields, kissing my babies and full-on belly laughs as they grew into toddlers riding on my shoulders. Others reminded me of the time we found love again and portrayed the joy of becoming a family of four once more when Brandon came into our lives.

My mind raced from wedding pictures to family fun as my lungs picked up speed from the news I was hearing. My feet danced back and forth before our hanging memories as I soaked in the fresh information. "Babe, come here. Sit down with me as you listen." My husband's voice was a mix of worry and grace as he watched my whole life crash before his eyes.

"No, I can't. Just let me hear him. So, it is what we thought, then? I have cancer?"

"Yes, sweetheart, you have cancer."

His eyes were wet from crying only moments before he broke the news, and my heart sank in disbelief. My hands clutched the computer as I turned the volume up on the recording. Bran received the phone call from my oncologist just an hour beforehand, and although my spirit knew what was fixing to take place, it wasn't easy to hear.

Only sixty minutes ago, the smell of fall filled our home, and my heart was full of encouragement. The girls were spending the night with my in-loves, and Brandon was preparing his famous pot of chili for a cook-off he was determined to win. I was hosting a Zoom call that night with about thirty women nationwide when Bran motioned to his phone and mouthed a silent, "It's the oncologist calling."

I knew then that what I was doing was more important than the news I would receive, and I signaled him to take the call without me. Our last mentoring session was through my first book, #Unfiltered, and a familiar scripture echoed through my mind, Matthew 8:21: *Another of the disciples said to Him, Lord, let me first go and bury my father. But Jesus said to him, 'Follow me, and allow the dead to bury their own dead.'* I never fully understood that passage until this moment. What I was imparting into these women far outweighed what awaited me at the end of that phone call. The news would be there when I was done. Sharing the good news of the Gospel was first.

The faces on the screen would have never known how real my words would become from that session: "Destiny is found in the dirt of your life. You must be willing to celebrate in the chaos, knowing that God is creating a future full of hope." I ended our mentorship that night, knowing that every lesson I coached these women through was fixing to be tested on a level I'd never known. #*Unfiltered* was resolving to become the reality of my life, and I'd have to make a choice about the dirt I was presented with.

My pace kept consistent, and my breath linked up to Dr. Williams' voice as I looked at my daughters' faces on the wall. "I normally don't give news like this on the phone, but you all are like family. I didn't want you waiting any longer, and I would typically wait for Alissa to be on this call. But since you are recording it for her and she's aware you're talking to me, the biopsy results did come back. She has invasive ductal carcinoma, grade 2. Now, this is different from staging. We won't know that until further tests are done, but we have a plan and will get through this."

The words after that became distant and faded into the rhythm of my breath, "No! I don't want this. I can't. My girls need me." Brandon grabbed my hand mid-pace and gently took the computer from my grasp. "God prepared you for this. Remember the promise you told me. This will not be unto death, but for the glory of the Lord. We must stand on that."

It's true; I was prepared for this moment months before any news became a recording on a device. My health hadn't been good for a while, and the Holy Spirit was so sweet to warn me of things to come while reminding me of the promise of His Word. Still, the words *breast cancer* pierced my heart as I processed the genuine reality of a devastating journey that awaited me. I don't remember much talking after that.

We sat on the couch with our fingers laced together as we fought to steady our thoughts. "Okay! Let's do something right now. Let's make a deal. How do we want to celebrate when all of this is over? Where do you want to go? We are going to concentrate on that, not the fight." I sat dazed by the flood of emotions hitting me in the gut, but the hope in my husband's eyes was enough for me to feel faith arise. "Alright, Bora Bora. I want to celebrate on clear water, in a hut, where worries aren't allowed in." He squeezed my hand and confidently declared, "Bora Bora it is. We will celebrate there soon!"

The night ended with a phone call to my parents who encouraged, prayed and prophesied a future of hope and destiny over me. They strengthened our faith as we learned to lean into a peace that surpassed all understanding. The kind of peace that Philippians 4:7 talks about. That's when it happened, friend, when I heard God say, *You'll fight this war with my Word in your mouth. I've never lost a battle.*

The following day, I did something that would shift the trajectory of my entire journey. It became the blueprint I'd follow daily and imprinted itself on my heart. The old saying, *Whose report will you believe? I will believe the report of the Lord!* rang out in my spirit. I told myself that I may not see it with my physical eyes, but I must believe so that my spiritual eyes could see a different outcome.

There was no crazy revelation that took place. Jesus didn't meet me in the middle of the night hour and share secrets from the heavenlies. No, it was simple and elementary regarding our walk with the Lord, yet it's neglected more than we'd like to admit. Friend, why wait until our life falls apart to begin a prayer life? Why do we only search for answers when it's too late? What makes us prepare for battle when we are already at war?

This goes far beyond cancer. This can be applied to every difficult situation that life throws your way. It may not be a disease for you; maybe it's depression. It could be the loss of a business or bankruptcy in your finances. Applying the simple steps I took can cover every area of your life. The trauma can stem from emotional, mental or spiritual roots, but the process is still the same.

* * *

Write it.

Before we move any further in this book, I want to allow you to assess where you're at in your journey. How can you address your next if you don't acknowledge your now? Put this book down and grab some paper and a pen; I will wait.

Now that you're back, please write down the areas in your world that feel like a fight. It could be anything: fear, anxiety, disease, relationships, finances, insecurity, addiction, health, depression, PTSD. There is no right or wrong answer. Take time to pray and ask the Holy Spirit to show you any hidden areas you have dismissed or accepted as normal. The goal here is to recognize the attacks to fight in faith correctly. Friend, if you're not aware of an issue, how can you address it?

I like to brain-dump everything on a page and then allow the Father to show me what to do with it. For me, that looks like a blank piece of paper and a timer on my phone. In two minutes or less, I dump every word, phrase and feeling I can think of concerning the topic at hand on the page. It's messy, scattered and chaotic, but it allows my mind to unload without wasting time overanalyzing the situation.

You can try this option and see how it works for you. Remember, you're not trying to find a solution. You're simply pinpointing your journey's location, like sharing your location on an iPhone. When you go to a contact and share your location, it gives you three options. You can share for an hour, 'til the end of the day or indefinitely.

When you permit the person, they can access where you are currently located, where you're headed and where you will end up. This is what we are doing with this activity. We are giving God the ability to assess where we are so that He can help us strategize and oversee where we are headed and where we end up. You have the authority to give Him access to this area of your life until the end of the day or indefinitely. I pray you take the challenges in this book and make it an indefinite decision. I promise you it will change your life. Now, take some time (maybe even a two-minute brain-dump) and *share your location* with the Father before you read further in this book.

***

When I woke up the following day, I grabbed my computer and did what most people do when they want to learn something: I pulled up Google. In the search bar, I typed out *healing scriptures* and copied and pasted every promise to a Word document titled #Unfiltered Fight. One thing I knew for sure that fighting was inevitable, but how I went about it was a choice. Any time unfortunate circumstances collide with life, we are presented with the opportunity to react in fear or respond in faith. Both are fighting stances, but only one wins the battle.

Contrary to your belief, fighting the good fight of faith can only be done with the Word of faith in your mouth. How can you speak without first knowing what to say? Friend, it's essential to understand what God says about your situation. You'll always get faith wrong if you don't get your mouth right. Your identity becomes rooted in the label you're facing, and fear will become your anchor if you're not careful. Everything changes when the

Word is planted in your heart, and your identity is rooted in faith.

I knew this to be true in my life. If faith comes by hearing and hearing the Word of God (Romans 10:17), then fear would come by hearing and hearing what my situation says. The following seven months of my life could be consumed with doctor appointments, treatments and the weekly rehearsing of a diagnosis that brings constant fear to life. If I was going to fight in faith, I'd have to fill my mouth with the Word of life. I'd have to guard my ears from death and keep my vision on what I could see spiritually rather than physically. You may ask, how is that even possible?

Maybe your situation seems impossible. It could be a physical struggle or an emotional battle. Perhaps you're reminded every day of the brokenness in your family or the lack of provision in your bank account. You could be mentally struggling to hold on to the hope that life is worth living. Or maybe you feel completely overwhelmed by so many things that you don't even know where to start. Perhaps the loss in your life is so heavy that you don't feel hope at all.

Before you can move forward in this process, you must understand one thing: for faith to come, you must hear, and before you can hear, you must speak. Friend, faith places a demand on your command. In other words, you can't have faith unless you speak up! Believe it or not, hearing is vital to what you believe in life. Life and death are in the power of your tongue (Proverbs 18:21), and it determines your fight stance. Will you react in fear or respond in faith?

I had to intentionally guard my ears by filling my mouth with words of faith, no matter what was in front of me. This took work. When I shared this truth with my husband, we both had to make a pact to keep our mouths accountable to God's Word. To do that, we had to prepare our mouths by positioning our eyes first. Did you know that your eyes will feed on what your mouth says? I found this to be true during this season of my life.

Matthew 6:22, AMP says, "The eye is the lamp of the body; so if your eye is clear [spiritually perceptive], your whole body will be full of light [benefiting from God's precepts]. But if your eye is bad [spiritually blind], your whole body will be full of darkness [devoid of God's precepts]. So if the very light inside you [your inner self, your heart, your conscience] is darkness, how great and terrible is that darkness!"

What you see will feed what you say, and what you say will determine what you believe. My goal when cancer hit was threefold. Say it, believe it, see it. I may not be able to see it physically, but what I see will determine what I believe, and what I believe will determine what I say. They are all linked together in a simple equation given to us in Mark 11:24, AMP: "For this reason I am telling you, whatever things you ask for in prayer [accordance with God's will], believe [with confident trust] that you have received them, and they will be given to you." In other words, if you say it, you will begin to believe it, and then you will start to see it first with your spiritual eyes and then with your physical. These are the three steps of faith to win the battle Jesus already won: speak, believe and see it.

The following day after being told, "You have cancer", I didn't see healing physically. Nothing had changed from the night before despite the prayers we prayed and the tears we cried. Still, I got up, googled references and made a Word document of over forty healing scriptures to place before my eyes. From there, I printed out fourteen of my favorite ones and taped them to my bathroom mirror. I created an index card ring with those same scriptures to throw in my purse, and then I made a vision board of twenty things that displayed the promise of healing regarding my future. I was intentional in what I saw because I understood it would feed my belief system and would ultimately determine what I'd say and see about my future.

Some might say this was overkill and that there's no real need to put in that level of effort. My question is, "Doing what you're doing now, how is your faith working for you?" My experience has shown me that faith without works is dead. If I wanted to see life from that fight, I had to work it.

I understood that if all I saw was disease and death, then my words could quickly become laced with diagnosis and discouragement. Friend, if life and death are found in the power of my tongue, then that tells me one thing: I have power, and so do you! Power equals control, and control is defined as "the power to influence or direct people's behavior or the course of events."[1] In other words, you may not be able to control what life throws at you, but you have the power to take control over what comes next.

I know what you're thinking, *Alissa, if I could control this situation, I would! This is completely out of my capability, and sometimes things happen that we can't change.* I get it. I have struggled with the same thought process, but can I tell you something? That's a lie! It's a trick of the enemy to keep you stuck in a fighting stance positioned in fear. And let me remind you, fear never wins a battle.

---

[1] Oxford Languages. June 2024.
https://www.google.com/search?q=definition+of+control

The truth is you may not have control over what is currently taking place in your life. I surely didn't have control over the cancer diagnosis of October 8th, 2020, and if I had, I would have made it all go away quickly. But what I discovered would change everything for me, and it will do the same for you if you grab ahold of the words on this page. There may be something in your life that you currently can't control, but there are three things you do have control over: what you speak, what you believe and what you see. Nothing will ever be able to take that away from you.

I don't know what your situation is at this moment. I won't try to pen the trauma, despair or pain you're enduring. I will ask you to take a second and picture your giant, whatever it may be, and give it a name. (It could be all the things you brain-dumped on your page earlier.)

David's giant was named Goliath; yours may be disease, depression, divorce, grief, lack, abuse or trauma. Whatever it's called, can you hear the lies it's been persuading you to believe? The first thing the Philistine told David was, "Am I a dog, that you come to me with [shepherd's] staffs? Come to me, and I will give your flesh to the birds of the sky and the beasts of the field" (1 Samuel 17:43-44, AMP). His goal was to paint a picture of fear with words so that David could see nothing but death in his future.

Notice, he hadn't yet died. Beasts or birds weren't physically eating his flesh, but Goliath's words came as an opportunity for David to see something that wasn't as though it was. Words are powerful, my friend. I wonder how your giant is lying to you. How is he telling your story? Is he feeding you a vision destined for nothing more than destruction? You may not be able to control the attack, but you can control the outcome.

Something I found empowering was David's response to the Philistine. "You come to me with a sword, a spear, and a javelin, but I come to you in the name of the Lord of hosts, the God of the armies of Israel, whom you have taunted. This day, the Lord will hand you over to me, and I will strike you down and cut off your head.

And I will give the corpses of the army of the Philistines this day to the birds of the sky and the wild beasts of the earth, so that all the earth may know that there is a God in Israel, and that this entire assembly may know that the Lord does not save with sword or with spear; for the battle is the Lord's and he will hand you over to us" (1 Samuel 17:45-47, AMP).

Did David allow what he couldn't control to control him? No, what did he do? He took control of the three things that no one could take away from him, and that no one can take away from *us*: what we speak, believe and see. Friend, your giant may be loud and clever with false imaginations, but you can choose what's next. What will your fight stance be? Will you react in fear or respond in faith? David responded in faith by replacing the threat with the truth of God's Word. He spoke what He knew about God, believed it was possible and saw it with his spiritual eyes.

Do you know what happened when David followed this three-step process in his own life? It allowed him the ability to run towards the enemy without fear. He slung a stone, stood over Goliath and cut his head off with the Philistine's own sword. David killed the champion and became the champion, all because he refused to allow fear to position him.

How will you face your giant? What will you see about your future? Will the words of your mouth agree with the threat or truth today? How are you fighting, and what do you want the outcome to be? You may not control the giant, but you can control *you*. I never said this would be easy, but I promise God never fails. If you take Mark 11:24 and apply the three steps to your life, you win. All you must do is speak, believe and see it.

* * *

Steps Towards Winning

Earlier, we took time to write down our fight by brain-dumping the tangible reality of our situations. I want to challenge you to find what God says about your reality this time. What truth words can you use to replace the threat that's standing in front of you? Type this in Google to help you find a starting point, "Bible scriptures on overcoming _____," (fill in the blank) with some target words from your brain-dump page. You'll find hundreds of articles, scriptures and teachings concerning your topic. Read and write down the references that speak loudly to your heart. I've included my list of healing scriptures for those fighting a physical battle in the back of this book. My website also has pre-made prayer card rings for different faith fights. So many people asked me to make these available once I began to teach on the power of God's Word in our mouth, and they have been a highly impactful tool for others in their journey toward winning.

You may want to create a Word document with a title representing your faith fight. Mine was titled, *#Unfiltered Faith Fight*; whatever you decide, get your scriptures together and keep them handy for your journey. After you have gathered your words, I want you to practice seeing or visualizing what you believe. I did this by taping scriptures to my mirror. I'd look myself in the eyes multiple times a day and declare one scripture after another out loud. I prophesied life over my body even when healing wasn't seen in the reflection looking back at me. I did this routine bald, frail and sicker than I've ever imagined I could be.

When lies came to attack my mind, I'd drag myself to the mirror and speak the Word. I'd look at my reflection while telling my giant what I saw in the spirit. Healing wasn't a possibility for me; it was a *guarantee* because God said it. Friend, get in front of your mirror and tell your giant what the outcome will be, and do it daily.

* * *

Pray it.

Father, thank You for allowing me to agree with what You've said about my story. I ask that You give me spiritual eyes to see what Your Word says over what my worry says. Although the circumstances might be extraordinary, I call the giant by name and say, "_____ (fill in the blank), you must bow your knee to the name of Jesus. You will not have power over my belief system and will not dictate to me my future. I speak to you now and declare that I win according to God's Word." Romans 8:28, NIV says, "All things work together for good to those who love God to bring about what is good." It's good in my life because God, You say so. And if You say it, I believe it, and that settles it. In Jesus' name, Amen.

Chapter 2

Hold Your Ground

Journal

10/21/2020

Hello,

My goodness, what a full 48 hours it has been; yesterday was "the day" that I've been dreading. We told our girls about everything and watched them weep. Kinsleigh is so strong and always bottles up her emotions. She will cry while putting on a brave face. Rory, on the other hand, fell to pieces.

When Bran & I picked them up from school, we took them to Dairy Queen for ice cream. It had been a long day with the oncologist, and our minds were still processing all the information from the afternoon. Regardless, I told B I wanted to tell the kids today and afterwards, our social media following. It's been a weight that I no longer wish to carry secretly.

When we got to Dairy Queen, I asked the Holy Spirit for the right words to say to the kids. It wasn't long before Kinsleigh opened the conversation with, "So what have y'all been doing all day?"

I responded with, "Well, you both know Mommy has been having problems with my breast, right? Well, today we went to the doctor to discuss what we're doing to fix it." The girls sat unbothered by the conversation as they innocently listened to me talk. "The imaging found a couple of lumps, and they say it's breast cancer." Immediately, the girls stopped licking their ice cream. With it dripping down their chins, they looked at me with big eyes and said, "What! Cancer?"

"Yes, babies, don't be scared. All cancer is different, and the level of cancer is different. Mommy is going to have to do some treatment where they give me medicine through an IV to help these lumps. We are praying and believing they will get smaller! God has given us great doctors who believe in Jesus, and I want you to know that God has got this! We're going to be okay."

Both looked unsure as they hesitated to eat any more of their treats. I knew I couldn't leave it at that. Bran and I made a promise to be transparent and honest with the girls through this process. "I want y'all to know that the meds they're giving me might make Mommy's hair fall out...." Before I could continue, Rory screamed out a panicked cry, "WHAT! No, no, no! I don't want that!"

At this point, Kins had tears streaming down her face while remaining determined to be brave. She's been my little protector since the divorce. Clearly, nothing has changed. Bran grabbed my hand and squeezed it as he began to weep silently.

Under my breath, I said a prayer, "Father, help me. I need peace and wisdom right now. This is the hardest thing I've ever done. Help me communicate this correctly." With one deep breath, I continued. "Girls, listen to me. It's only hair, sweethearts. It's not forever. It's just for now. It will grow back with time, and we will try to have fun with this, okay?! You will get to help me cut, color and shave it off. We can even go pick out wigs and head wraps together! God's got this, I promise."

Rory wasn't having it and shouted, "Let's just get you a wig that looks like your hair now. Let's keep this a secret! No one has to know! Please don't let anyone know." Through tears, she whispered, "It's our secret, Mommy."

My heart shattered into a million pieces with my husband, "Baby, it can't be a secret. I have to show people Jesus through this...."

She interrupted, "I don't want to tell anyone! I don't want your hair to go away!" I watched Rory's heart breaking into a thousand pieces before me as Kins looked out the window, trying to hold it together. I could see Kins' brain spinning as she blurted out, "Do people die of breast cancer?"

"Kins, stop talking! I don't want to know if she'll die! I don't want to know any more! Please, can we stop talking?!"

My heart strings couldn't handle all the emotions whaling me in the small space of our car. At this point, Bran was looking out the window with tear-stained cheeks. He sat covering his mouth in fear of letting out a cry of sorrow, and all I could do was squeeze his hand even tighter in hopes of comforting him. I looked back at my girls who, just minutes before, had messy hair from a busy day at school, ice cream on their chins and joy in their eyes. Moments later, they were wrapped up in confusion, fear and anger as their ice cream melted and their eyes ran streams of pain. *God, I need You here with us right now. You told us to be honest with them, but now I don't know. Please help us at this moment.*

Before I could think about it, words began to spill out of my mouth. "Girls, I'm not dying! God has this! He's bigger than cancer! I'm healed, and I'm not going anywhere! It's going to be a journey, but we will find joy in it! We will be okay, and you will watch a miracle!" Instantly, I started to silently pray. *You have this, God. Don't let me down for the sake of my girls. I believe You're who You say You are. Now, let's shake Hell together.* Bran dried his eyes and turned to address the girls, "Babies, we have always made it our honor to share Jesus through every season of our life. People around the world will watch a miracle through this. We believe God is greater than cancer."

As they processed everything being said, Rory shrugged her shoulders and said, "Maybe we can get a Minnie Mouse scarf for your head and a purple wig?" We all smiled through our tears as I pulled up Amazon and winked, "Here, go ahead and pick out all the things; we have to make sure Mommy looks good while fighting this."

Later that evening, I scheduled a hair appointment to start cutting my hair in stages. I wanted to prepare the girls for such a huge transition. My hair was so long, and the idea of losing it all was a big concern for Rory. I wanted to do everything possible to help them through it as smoothly as possible. Bran and I decided, after much prayer, that we get the opportunity to create the narrative here. Cancer can bring fear, but CHRIST brings peace. We decided not to overload the girls with information, but we wanted them to know the truth so that they could see the miracle as it unfolds. I didn't want to withhold the bad, scary and uncomfortable details. I wanted them to learn faith through this situation and come out saying, "God is who He says He is! He never fails!"

We made phone calls telling family and friends that night, and then we went live to share our news with the world. Everyone was super supportive and showed solidarity with us.

God called me to live life #*Unfiltered,* out loud, in the open, so I wanted to show my girls how to do that. I wanted to show them that God always keeps His promises and that we should always trust Him with our pain. My prayer was that God will protect them from fear and worry; that childlike faith would rise within them, and they'd encounter Jesus in ways they had never imagined during this time.

Kinsleigh and Aurora are my heartbeats, the exclamation points to my story. They are the reason my face knows joy, and my soul knows love. As a parent, my heart broke to put them through that. I never wanted to be the cause of pain in their life. I wanted to protect them, but I knew God would protect them better. He could love them better. I knew that they would watch me walk in my purpose and celebrate the WIN with me in the end because God is faithful to keep His word.

I'm reading my healing scriptures three times a day (since I started a month ago). I believe that it's finished, and I declare that I win!

It is well because it is done.

-*Alissa*

We stepped into the cancer center hand in hand as the unknown lingered over our heads. I intentionally wore my *waymaker, miracle worker, and promise keeper* shirt as a reminder that God was in control, and I grabbed a mask to match. It was hard enough being diagnosed at 31 years young, but doing so smack dab in the middle of a pandemic, added extra stress to the situation. Still, I was thankful Bran could be with me for this appointment. I didn't realize it at the time, but I'd go through every scan, infusion and doctor's visit alone due to COVID restrictions.

When we checked in at the front desk, we reluctantly sat down, waiting impatiently for the nurse to call us back. I couldn't help but notice the silver heads lining the waiting room, and they all stared our way, questioning who the young couple in the room was. Everyone there seemed to be 65 years of age and over; surely, I wasn't the youngest in the center. The looks I received were a mix of shock and sadness. I'm sure they all wondered what I was doing in the center and where our elderly patient was. Once they called my name, we glanced at each other with silent words of encouragement, knowing that both of us were terrified of what we'd hear. This was the day that the chemotherapy plan would be put in motion, and we'd leave having a better understanding of just how long this journey would last.

When the oncologist walked into the room, his words were straightforward and matter-of-fact. "Mrs. Holt, it seems you have stage 1b invasive ductal carcinoma estrogen and progesterone positive, but you're HER2 negative. With you being so young, we want to treat this as aggressively as possible. That being said, I'll be putting you on sixteen rounds of a chemotherapy plan called AC-T. It includes four rounds of Adriamycin and cyclophosphamide and twelve rounds of Taxol.

"Mrs. Holt, this chemotherapy is tough, but we believe it's necessary with your age. It will take about five to six months to complete as long as there are no complications. You will lose your hair, but it will grow back. There will be many side effects and changes, but the nurses will review all of that with you for your start. We will also be putting you into medically induced menopause to stop the production of estrogen in your body. We hope to preserve your egg health with it.

"Your cancer is estrogen-driven, and it is essential to start this immediately. Although everything will start very fast, we will take it one step at a time. Dr. Williams will schedule further scans and surgery to place your port for treatments. This chemo is very toxic and cannot be put directly into your veins. The next two weeks will be full, but we want to start soon. Do you have any questions for me?"

I don't want my hair to go away, rang through my mind as I squeezed Bran's hand for support. Did I have any questions? I had lots of questions, but where would I even start? I searched my husband's face for the words that wouldn't come out of my mouth. Eventually, he squeezed my hand, reminding me to talk, and I replied, "No, I think you've covered it." After all, what good would it do me to sit and question everything he said? This is where we were in life, and I was ready to get it on with it so we could move forward.

From there, I was given a physical exam and we were sent on our way with a load of information, a heavy cloud looming overhead. When I approached the check-out desk, the secretary printed out my first chemotherapy appointment reminder and handed it to me. My stomach felt like I'd eaten rocks for breakfast, and the older man beside me shot a *I'm so sorry* look my way.

"Will my husband be able to assist me with my infusions?" I intently searched the secretary's face for comfort but couldn't see past her stupid mask. "No, I'm sorry. COVID restrictions do not allow patients to have any visitors. We aren't supposed to allow anyone back to your doctor appointments, but it was your first visit, so we made an exception." Fear gripped my heart, as I'm sure the color left my face. "Really? Cancer is terrifying. Why would y'all make me do this alone?" She looked up from her computer and gently said, "I know this is, but you'll have nurses here with you. I promise you won't be alone."

They don't know me, though. It isn't the same as having family there to calm my nerves and to pray with me if something goes wrong. I don't want strangers to support me through this. I need my husband. This has got to be a nightmare. I could tell I wouldn't win the argument, so I let my thoughts scream inside my head as I pushed the door open to exit the center. A waiting room full of elderly eyes met me with sympathy and questioning looks.

Why am I here? Is this really my life? My husband pulled the car up, and I quickly got in. Anger vibrated in my tone, "You're not allowed to be with me for my treatment. I have to do this all alone! They don't even care. They said I'd have nurses to help me. But it's not the same!" Brandon grabbed my hand and whispered peace into my heart. "I'm so sorry, love. I hate this for you and wish I could do it for you; if it could be me, I'd take it all away. Just remember, I may not be with you, but Jesus is always there. He will get you through this."

Immediately, I remembered the dream I had the night before. It was a beautiful display of healing as I watched God create a movement with a mountain in the dream. I heard his voice speak so clearly: *Cancer can't move its feet physically until you move your feet spiritually.* I woke up to the vision board hanging on my wall, and it reminded me why faith must remain intact. "Father, what do You mean my feet must move spiritually?" Without any time to process, I saw a picture in my mind's eye of myself standing resolutely, wearing a complete set of armor. Ephesians 6 was brought to mind, and I jumped out of bed to grab my Bible to read it:

> "Put on the full armor of God [for His precepts are like the splendid armor of a heavily-armed soldier], so that you may be able to

[successfully] stand up against all the schemes and the strategies and the deceits of the devil. For our struggle is not against flesh and blood [contending only with physical opponents], but against the rulers, against the powers, against the world forces of this [present] darkness, against the spiritual forces of wickedness in the heavenly (supernatural) places. Therefore, put on the complete armor of God so that you will be able to [successfully] resist and stand your ground in the evil day [of danger], and having done everything [that the crisis demands], to stand firm [in your place, fully prepared, immovable, victorious]. So stand firm and hold your ground, having tightened the wide band of truth (personal integrity, moral courage) around your waist, having put on the breastplate of righteousness (an upright heart), and having strapped on your feet the gospel of peace in preparation [to face the enemy with firm-footed stability and the readiness produced by the good

55

news]. Above all, lift up the [protective] shield of faith with which you can extinguish all the flaming arrows of the evil one. And take the helmet of salvation and the sword of the spirit, which is the Word of God."

- Ephesians 6:11-17, AMP

Friend, let me tell you a secret: you can't win a battle sitting down. David had to stand firm in battle before he could hold the giant's severed head in his hands. How did he do that? By holding his ground with the Word of God in his mouth. In other words, your ability to hold the head of victory will stem from your ability to hold your ground in battle. You can't see a win if you never get up to fight, and your ability to stand is directly affected by your decision to prepare. Look at what the Word says again, "So stand firm and hold your ground, having tightened the wide band of truth (personal integrity, moral courage) around your waist and having put on the breastplate of righteousness (an upright heart), and having strapped on your feet the gospel of peace in preparation [to face the enemy with firm-footed stability and the readiness produced by the good news]."

What exactly is the belt of truth? It's the first piece of the armor, so it must be important, right? John 14:6 says that Jesus is the way, the truth and the life, and we only come to know God through Him. The rest of the armor wouldn't work without the truth because we'd lack understanding to hold firm to it.

In my twenties, I had the honor of pastoring a church in Texas alongside my parents. On my dad's bookshelf sat a figurine of the whole armor of God. I remember studying the significance of the representation and was shocked at the importance of something as small as a belt.

Let me help bring clarity to this passage of scripture. Ephesians was written by a disciple named Paul, and he described the armor of God to look much like that of a Roman soldier who was ready for battle, only the belt of a Roman soldier in Jesus' day was not like our typical leather strap. It was thick and had a heavy metal on a leather band that contained a protective piece hanging down from the front. It was primarily used to hold the soldier's sword and other weapons that he might carry.

When we picture it the way Paul describes, we then understand that the belt of truth is directly connected to the sword of the Spirit, representing the Word of God. John 1:1 says, "In the beginning was the Word, and the Word was with God, and the Word was God." In other words, the first thing Paul tells us to put on is the truth of Jesus, and the last thing he tells us to put on is the Word of God.

Friend, you have no chance to hold your ground if you have no understanding of two particular things. One, who Jesus is in your life, and two, what His Word says about you. He is the truth that surrounds you, guarding your innermost being, and His Word is what you utilize to fight in faith. Every other part of the armor mentioned in Scripture is sandwiched between those two foundations. What that tells me is that an upright heart (breastplate of righteousness), peace (feet), faith (shield) and mind (helmet) come into alignment with the truth (belt) and Word (sword)!

Saying, believing and seeing cannot result in a victory if you're not holding your ground with understanding who Christ is and what His Word says. When God spoke that cancer couldn't move its feet physically until I move my feet spiritually, He was saying that I must put on the armor and hold my ground! Verse 15 of Ephesians 6 says, "And having strapped on your feet the gospel of peace in preparation [to face the enemy with firm-footed stability and the readiness produced by the good news]." *So, Alissa, how do we hold our ground?* Friend, we stand firm on the truth and prepare our feet with the gospel of peace.

In simpler terms, to face the enemy, you must be firm-footed in the Word and ready with the Word at all times. I'm reminded of the story about Jesus in the wilderness. He had been fasting for forty days and forty nights and was hungry, tired and weak when satan came to tempt him in Matthew 4, AMP: "And the tempter came and said to him, 'If you are the Son of God, command that these stones become bread.' But Jesus replied, 'It is written and forever remains written; man shall not live by bread alone but by every word that comes out of the mouth of God.'"

A couple of verses down, satan begins to mock Jesus, saying, "Throw yourself off a cliff and command your angels to protect you" (v.6). Jesus once again replied with, "It is written and quoted the verse, "You shall not test the Lord your God." The tempter then took Him to a very high mountain and showed Him all the world's kingdoms. He began telling Jesus that he'd give Him all of it if He only fell and worshiped him. Still, Jesus responded, "It is written..." and quoted, "You shall worship the Lord your God and serve Him only."

Hear me, friend: physical movement is recognized with the eye, but spiritual movement is exercised by the mouth. If you want to hold your ground, **"It is written..."** *must* be your declaration. Stop allowing yourself to give up so quickly! You have to tap into your righteous anger and HOLD ON!

* * *

Write it.

Okay, friend, it's time to journal. I also want to encourage you to think of the pages of this book as your designated FIGHT journal! If it weren't for writing the history of my story with Jesus, I'm not sure I'd even be writing this book. My ability to look over the process has allowed me to push through and continue fighting in faith, and I believe it will be the same for you!

So here's your homework: I want to challenge you to begin writing declarations about your story. Spiritual movement is exercised by the mouth, but how can you intentionally fight if you don't take time to strategize? I've been disciplined with faith not because it's easy, but because I've nurtured my consistency to it. Friend, I made it EASY. The fight is hard enough, so why make it harder? So how did I do it? By saying the SAME THINGS every day. I pulled out my truth words (scriptures) and spoke them OUTLOUD. I flipped through my declarations and listened to my MOUTH hold my ground spiritually. Remember, battles are won because of precision and discipline. It takes action to make it happen!

Here is where you make it personal. The goal is to write positive truths about what God says concerning your situation. You may not see it, but you'll say it anyway. Pray and ask the Holy Spirit to help you speak LIFE over your fight. Here are some ideas:

I am forever healed.

I am equipped for this season.

I win because Jesus won.

Peace is my pillow.

* * *

* * *

When we drove away from the cancer center, something arose within my spirit on the way home. The fight of faith is something I'd never spiritually felt before, but this time, I knew it was different; losing wasn't an option.

You see, I was part of a Girl Scouts club when I was ten. Many outdoor activities allowed us to earn badges. One day, horse riding was on the agenda. I'll never forget that fall afternoon in the woods of Arkansas. The leaves were changing colors and the air was crisp. I was standing in line outside a log cabin, waiting my turn to climb onto the back of my new friend. I'd never met a horse before, but it seemed easy enough, or so I thought.

Before I knew it, my turn arrived, and the scout leader gave me a hand up onto my saddle. With both hands gripping the reins, I effortlessly glided across the field. Slowly, we made our way to the fence and were heading back when my horse caught sight of a snake on the ground. Immediately, my hands found their way to my saddle horn and the horse began to buck around with me on its back.

Terrified and holding on for dear life, the scout leader ran my way, screaming, "Hold on tight! He's scared of something he saw, but you are still in control!" *Am I still in control? How? I'm sitting on the back of a monster whose strength overpowers anything a ten-year-old girl could compete with!*

Maybe you feel this way right now. You're sitting on the back of a beast that's violently throwing you around, and you're desperately clinging to hope while trying to remain unharmed. Let me remind you, that beast is scared of something it saw and you are still in control!

Once my scout leader reached my side, she immediately did a one-rein stop. His hind legs became disengaged from bucking by bending his head and neck to one side, and authority was placed back into her hands. Before I could dismount the horse, she took my hand and put it on the rein with her. "Sometimes they see something that makes them buck, but you have the power to hold on, turn their head and control the outcome."

Friend, I don't know what is *bucking* in your life right now, but I am here to tell you that it's because the enemy saw something he feared. You have authority inside of you that he's trying to challenge, and it's your job to recognize the power struggle not because you're weak, but because the Word of God in you has made you strong. When destruction comes bucking, your response should be to hold on! You do that by attaching yourself to the truth of who Jesus is in your life and by activating your faith (sword), which is His Word. When you respond with, *It is written*, you turn the enemy's head towards defeat and disengage the attack on your life. You have been given the authority to control the outcome. The question is, will you hold on long enough to see it through?

When Bran and I decided to share this journey with our kids openly, we chose to create the narrative. Cancer may have won many battles, but Jesus never lost one. With the Word of God in our mouths, we held our ground, even when it felt like the pink monster was winning. Losing wasn't an option for us, and we stood by the belief that God's Word could not fail. If God said it, I believe it, and that's what I'm anchored to! Nothing could convince me to loosen my grip. No doctor's report, scan, chemotherapy reaction, pain or amount of hair falling out of my head could change my mind. I had fully convinced myself that His Word was the final say in my life, and because of that, it proved true.

Alissa, you've got to be kidding me. Manifesting the future is not real life. You can't speak words and see it change reality. This is a lot deeper than you're trying to make it. I hear you and you're right; it *is* much deeper than that. Throughout this book, I'm going to challenge you to stop fighting a war with surface-level prayers and fights. Friend, I'm charging you to dig deeper with faith by activating your authority. If you want to hold the giant's head in your hands, you've got to cut its throat.

In other words, you must silence the voice of defeat in your life by giving power to the voice of victory! The Word of God in your mouth will become the greatest weapon you could ever win with. David immediately created the narrative with the Philistine by holding on, turning his head towards the reality of who God is and controlling the outcome. He silenced the threat by proving the truth of who our God is.

Friend, stop listening to the lies and stop focusing on the fight. If you'll hold on, your faith will not fail you! How are you listening to the truth in God's Word more than the threat of your current situation?

* * *

Steps Towards Winning

Before we can move on, you must ask yourself the question, what are the reasons you want to win this fight of faith? Words create pictures, and what you speak will begin to paint a vision of what you believe about your situation. I want to take it further by challenging you to go to

Google again. Search images that represent what you'd like to see your life become. Is it a home that you own? Is it a business idea? A clean bill of health? Maybe you want children in the future or joy in your household. Find photos that represent those promises and print them out. Create a vision board that displays the things you are fighting for and believing are yours according to the Word. I found pictures of twenty things I wanted within the next ten years of my life, attached them to the board and hung it in my room. I knew that I'd be spending a lot of time in bed due to chemotherapy, so I wanted a visual reminder of what I was standing in faith for. Habakkuk 2:2, KJV says to "write the vision and make it plain." Be clear with what you want and hang it up as a daily reminder of faith.

* * *

Pray it.

Father, I thank You for intentional fighting and for allowing me to be disciplined in my belief system by remaining firm with the Word on my lips. I thank You for the strength I need to hold my ground when I feel weak. Allow me to replace the enemy's lies with the truth of what You say concerning my situation. Please help me to see what You see in me and continue to reveal all the areas that need to be uprooted and replaced with Your promises. I declare that I win this fight in Jesus' name because Christ already won! Amen.

Chapter 3

Capacity

Journal

10/27/2020

Hello,

This past weekend has been such a breath of fresh air. God was in the midst of it all, and He is creating a movement with this mountain. Some of our followers provided our family with the opportunity to go to Orlando and stay at a resort for three days. We desperately needed some family time before chemotherapy starts because I'm sure our world will become very disrupted. While there, we spent lots of time soaking in the sun, making memories, laughing, snuggling and being intentional with putting the electronics down. Staying present in the moment was our goal and our family is incredibly thankful for those who gave us this special getaway.

On our last day at the resort, I was due for a biopsy at my oncologist's office. When I was initially diagnosed, they found two masses in my left breast along with a suspicious lymph node. After the first biopsy of one tumor tested positive for two types of breast cancer, invasive ductal carcinoma and ductal carcinoma in situ, my doctor decided to test the other areas to be sure it was all the same thing. I was so scared because I had an awful experience with the first procedure due to the shingles I developed on my chest. It was so incredibly painful and left me a bit traumatized.

When I went into the office, I said a simple prayer at the door before I entered, *Father, allow this not to hurt. Let me receive negative results and confirm that what they thought they saw, they'll see no more.* I continued to stand on a Word my family and I were speaking, *Although it's there-it's not there in Jesus' name.* I was ready for whatever, but I kept the Word in my mouth. When the doctor came in for the procedure, he had a smile on his face and said, "I have good news! Your genetic testing has come in! It's negative! We tested it for 84 genes, and all of them came back negative!"

But God!

This means that I didn't have to worry about my family being at risk for breast cancer. My girls, sisters, nieces- they're all safe! This also meant that my right breast was not at-risk for disease. One breast was saved... now it was time to save the other. I continued to say that I would lose nothing, knowing that God is and would be faithful.

Once I laid down on the table to proceed with the two biopsies for the day (one on a tumor and the other on the lymph node), my heart began to race. "Father, I thank You I'll have no pain. These are coming back negative. I trust You." After ten to fifteen minutes of the doctor looking for the 2.1cm mass with an ultrasound machine, I noticed it was taking an unusual amount of time. With confusion on his face, I laid there remembering a Word that we received only six days prior from a man named Mark Filkey: "They've either misdiagnosed or they're going to find out it is less than they thought. God is doing a work in Alissa's body. You're fixing to get some good news."

I have been taught to always press record on my voice memos when someone is giving me a prophetic word. My father flows heavily in the prophetic gifting, and I know it's important to hear what God has spoken more than once to build faith. I'm so thankful that I had the recording in my phone electronically time stamped as a reminder of how good He truly is. I laid there recalling every word Mark spoke. I already received good news with the genetic test, and concerning the rest, I responded with a soft, "Ok God, prove it to be true."

Finally, after searching for a long while, the doctor spoke up, "Well, I can't seem to find that other mass. I still see the top mass. I even see the lymph node, but I can't find the other tumor. Sometimes radiology can see things I can't, but we'll have to have the MRI to see where it is." Immediately I heard in my spirit, "I told you so." God is a promise keeper.

Bran was sitting in the room with us. I was so grateful he could be a part in spite of COVID restrictions. He spoke up with a smile on his face, "So what are the chances a mass just disappears, Doc?" Dr. Williams replied with, "Ah, about 5%. That's why we will have to look at this on the MRI." I laid on the bed thinking to myself I am a part of the 5%. It is gone. This was a miracle.

We proceeded with a biopsy on the lymph node, and I felt zero pain during the procedure. I continued to believe everything would be negative in pathology. The doctor explained our next steps in detail once he was finished. "If the other mass isn't there in the MRI, and if this lymph node comes back negative, there's a chance we can save this breast with chemotherapy."

Operation Save My Other Breast had commenced. God is faithful. I will lose nothing, I said to myself. Our girls were in the waiting room, anxious to hear how it went for me. When we left the office, we sat as a family in the hospital lobby and shared every detail of the experience with them. Our hearts for them were to be honest and open throughout this journey so that they could celebrate the victories and miracles with us from a place of understanding.

Faith is not fair, it's a fight, and they needed to learn the reality of what that looked like. After telling them the news, they jumped up and down with tears in their eyes screaming, "It's really gone?! Jesus took the tumor out of Mommy?! Genetic testing is negative! We are so happy!" The four of us embraced each other as we celebrated the WIN. I'm believing that the MRI will confirm the mass is gone and that I've joined the 5% crew in miracles! God can and I believe!

-Alissa

Sometimes we learn how to walk in faith from others' journeys so that we can grow in our own faith and then walk it out on our own. It's by taking notes from someone else's faith walk that my life changed forever, branding my heart with the belief that if God could do it for her, then He could do it for me.

It was a hot ordinary summer day at my parents' house. My momma asked me to come help her prepare dinner for the crew that evening. My toddlers were watching a TV show in the living room when one of their favorite songs began to play, and almost immediately little feet pranced around the room in ballet twirls while bouncing motions vibrated across the floor.

We laughed as their faces scrunched up with expression and decided a dance break was in order for us all. With a kitchen towel draped over my momma's shoulder, two little hands made their way into hers. Twirling and laughing they took turns galloping around the room without a care in the world.

Everything was seemingly perfect at that moment. Food was cooking, family was waiting to gather and belly laughs filled the air. That's when everything changed. From giggles to groans, I watched my momma's face shift from careless joy to painstaking fear. She moved to the couch to catch her breath and tried to lay down while clutching her abdomen. "Are you ok?" I asked. "Yes, I just have a catch in my stomach. I'll be fine."

Before I could make my way back to the kitchen, I noticed she was no longer in the room with us. Something wasn't right and I felt it in my gut. One thing I knew for sure, Veronica Powers is not the kind of woman to show discomfort of any kind. Being tough was a part of her DNA and if pain was present in her life, well, none of us ever knew about it.

Making my way down the hall, I could hear her vomiting in the bathroom. When I rounded the corner, it only took a split second for me to decide what needed to be done. "Mom, we are going to the hospital now. Your face is so pale there's no color left! Do you want an ambulance or for me to drive? You need to decide now because we are going!" My heart pounded as my grandmother came to help me get her off the floor. We listened to her cries repeatedly whisper one word alone, *Jesus.* I'd never seen her like this before in my life, but I knew it was serious. Barely able to communicate, I drove her to the emergency room as she whispered, "Don't hit bumps. Jesus, help me."

It took hours of sitting in that waiting room for us to hear anything. My sisters and I sat praying as my grandmother worshiped alongside us. When Daddy came out, tears filled his eyes. We grabbed each other's hands and swallowed the lumps in our throat as we waited for him to share the news. What in the world was happening? We were just cooking and dancing! How could this be?

Leading us down the hallway, his voice spoke with authority despite the tears, "I want to start by reminding you of the story of the umpire. Do you remember it?" This was a story we heard from a pastor friend that pricked our hearts in such a way it became a family mantra for the Powers clan.

He continued, "The batter came up to base and the pitcher made his throw. With the throw of the ball, the batter failed to swing, and the crowd waited for the umpire's call. With no call being made, the players began to ask, "Ump, what is it?" With no response the crowd began to say, "Ump, what is it?" Still, with no call being made the pitcher began to scream, "Ump, make the call!" Finally, the ump said, 'It ain't nothing 'til I call it something!' The umpire had the final say in the game.

"Girls, your mom looked at me in the room back there and said it ain't nothing 'til I call it something, and I call it what the Word says. God has the final say and that's what we are believing. So, we don't want to hear anything other than what we say we are calling it. Do you understand?"

Terrified of what we'd hear next, we agreed to speak only the Word over my momma. God makes the final call in the game. It didn't matter what others saw and what they thought, He was the one we listened to. "Your mom has a tumor the size of a cantaloupe on her ovary. It seems to be mobile and has flipped her fallopian tube upside down. That's what caused her extreme pain and discomfort. They are trying to say that this is cancer, but it ain't nothing 'til we call it something. We call it healed. We call it benign. That's what we believe. She has emergency surgery tomorrow and we will wait for God to confirm it through pathology in about a week."

My momma went into surgery early the next morning and although she left with an incision seven plus inches long, things went beautifully. The doctor said the tumor was the size of a baby. They weren't sure if it'd be attached to anything, but found they were able to lift it out without damaging any other area of her body.

For a week, we put our mouth on the belief that God would be faithful to His Word. Despite what they thought they saw, we called her healed and we didn't sway from our confession. When pathology came back, the doctors were shocked, and our family celebrated the benign report that she was cancer-free!

I didn't realize it at the time, but this day would prepare me for my own faith walk. *What they thought they saw, they'll see no more*, was a declaration from the lesson I watched my mom walk through in front of me nearly a decade prior to my journey. Friend, can I tell you, faith doesn't seem logical when paper proof states something different. Maybe you have a diagnosis of your own or maybe the papers are the proof of a failed marriage. Your papers could show the lack of provision in your life, or the failure of a career. Still, the question remains: whose report will you believe? What will YOU call it? It ain't nothing until you call it something.

* * *

Write it.

Time to grab that paper and pen, my friend. As an expecting mom, I recall how seriously I took the job of brainstorming my babies' names. I'd have pages of possibilities paired together spread out all over the table. I took time to say them out loud, write them in cursive and pray over which one fit perfectly for the baby I was expecting. I didn't want any ole name, I needed something that struck me with purpose.

I don't know if you're aware of this, but names carry so much power. In fact, they are so significant that God changed Sarai's name to Sarah, Abram to Abraham and Saul to Paul. He knew that new seasons required new signatures because what you sign your name to, is what you agree on. I wonder if you've truly taken time to acknowledge the name you've given your circumstance? Maybe a name change is required for this new journey.

I can remember the excitement I had as I prepared for my wedding day. The honor to take on the name *Holt* carried so much meaning and love. But it also required stepping away from the name that marked me much of my life. I had to separate from what I once identified with and come into a new identity. The completion of this process was the name change.

I want you to recognize the same process when it comes to your journey. If you want to agree with something new, you have to separate from the old way of identifying your situation. What will you call it? What label are you going to put on this issue?

Take time to write down the names you have been agreeing with and write the new name beside it! For example, your situation may be cancer, but today you name it *healed*. Maybe it's a broken spirit that you've clung to, but today you're naming it *whole*. You could be in lack, but the new name is now *abundance*. Get creative, speak the promise of what God says and find the power behind the agreement. It ain't nothing until you call it something.

* * *

Over the last two years of my life, I've had the opportunity to share many moments through cancer that were completely raw and vulnerable. Be it live feed or private moments released on YouTube, response messages never failed to make their way into my inbox. So many penned similar responses by making statements like, "You're so strong. I could never get through this the way you are." "How do you stay so positive? I feel like I'm failing." "Your faith is so inspiring. I don't know how you do it." And each time I'd share my secret with them in love by sending this scripture that changed my life forever.

"Yet we have the same spirit of faith as he had, who wrote in Scripture, 'I believed; therefore I spoke.' We also believe; therefore we also speak."

- 2 Corinthians 4:13, AMP

Friend, I don't have to know your giant by name, because I know the name that is above every name. I don't have to understand the circumstances you're facing, because I know the One who empowers us to WIN. I know we want the secret in becoming undefeated to be as easy as having some magical formula, but the reality is we fail to recognize the answer because we're too busy looking at the appearance.

Here's the truth, I don't have anything available to me that you don't have available to you. The scripture above says that we have the same spirit of faith accessible to us. That means my faith isn't any bigger than yours and your faith isn't bigger than mine. It isn't determined by circumstantial preferences or weighed on a scale of one to ten. It's simple, I believe so I speak.

Maybe you're not seeing results in your faith because the giant in your mind has caged the confession of your mouth. Or maybe the inability to shut your mouth to lies has encaged your mind to false realities. Regardless, your mind and mouth play a huge role on your faith walk. Remember, when everything feels out of control, those are the things we must remain in control of. The problem isn't that I have more faith than you, it's possible that you haven't learned the balance between belief and speech. It's not that I'm more capable than you are, it's possible that you may be participating in fear more than you're practicing faith. It's the measure in which you use belief and speech that will determine how you win this fight.

"For I say, through the grace given unto me, to every man that is among you, not to think of himself more highly than he ought to think; but to think soberly, according as God hath dealt to every man the measure of faith."

- Romans 12:3, KJV

I encourage you to read the entire twelfth chapter of Romans as it explains the many giftings we have as Christians, but what I want to zero in on is this simple truth: although the giftings may be different, the measure to utilize them correctly remains the same.

It's interesting to me that the Word doesn't say we've been given *a* measure of faith, but distinctly says we've been given *the* measure of faith. When diving into the Greek meaning of the word *measure* used in this scripture, I learned that the word was translated to *metron,* meaning an instrument for measuring. One definition even says that it's the vessel for receiving and determining the quantity of things. In other words, we (the vessel) are what measures faith in our life.[2]

We've been given the authority to choose how much or how little faith we carry with us on a daily basis. It isn't that I've been given more of it than you have, it's that I've chosen to live my life full of faith and sure of God's Word. I've realized that I'm the instrument that determines the measure that I carry, and I choose to think of God more than myself.

You may be saying, "Alissa, how do we determine how full our faith is when life is telling us otherwise?" Well, it's

[2] Blue Letter Bible. July 2024. Blue Letter Bible, 2024. https://www.blueletterbible.org/search/search.cfm?Criteria=measure&t=KJV#s=s_primary_0_1

simple really. I tell the ladies that I coach, "You have what you hear because you believe what you say." If 2 Corinthians 4:13 tells us that belief and speaking go hand in hand, then it only makes sense to know hearing will play a part in that as well.

Remember, Romans 10:17, KJV: "Faith comes by hearing and hearing by the word of God." Friend, hearing opens the door to having, but before anyone can hear, something must be spoken. Listening is the key to believing and receiving lies within your mouth. Your tongue must speak the truth of God's Word! The problem is that we have a low measurement of faith because our ears aren't hearing the Word, they're hearing our worries. We aren't declaring the promise; we're rehearsing the pain. We have put our mouth on the mountain with mourning instead of speaking to the mountain in faith, commanding it to move (Mark 11:23)!

Your voice is the most heard voice your ears will hear in your lifetime. The power of your words will determine the measurement of your faith. Don't believe me?

"Death and life are in the power of the tongue, and those who love it and indulge it will eat its fruit and bear the consequences of their words."

- Proverbs 18:21, AMP

I tell my ladies all the time, if I attached two buckets to either of your sides and labeled one life and the other death, I wonder which one would be fuller at the end of the day? Every word we speak is filling up the measure of our faith or depleting the measure with fear. We are responsible for the fulfillment of it by being intentional with the words of our mouth.

Remember, faith is activated by hearing, and belief is activated by speaking. In simple terms, we have not because we ask not. We say we want one thing, but our mouth says otherwise. We want a faith-filled life that's overflowing, but we consistently deplete our measure by making agreements with fear. Friend, remember the ump? It's time for you to decide what you want to call your situation. Are you agreeing with the paper proof or are you going to stick with the red letters of God's Word?

When I walked through this journey, there were many days that proof came to deplete the promise of healing in my life. That's when I recognized the voice of fear and redirected my belief system to faith. I shifted my eyes from the symptoms to my vision board. I allowed my words to be filled with the life of God rather than the death of cancer. I had to utilize the filling of my measurement so that it could serve me when I needed a drink of hope.

Let me ask you, how can you fight 'til the end if you're running on empty? So many give up in the middle of a battle because they've run out of faith to endure! If we keep our gas tank full on a road trip, then we must keep our faith tank full when we are on a journey towards winning! The measure in our tank will determine how far we can make it.

I can plan a cross country trip, but I won't make it to the destination if I don't consider the *number of times* I'll need to fill up! Friend, faith isn't just about fighting, it's equally about filling! If we don't take time to fill up the measure of our gas tank, then we will find ourselves sitting on the side of the road, empty and waiting for someone to pull over and help us. Don't put yourself in that position spiritually!

You have the same spirit of faith as anyone else does! You have the ability to fill up frequently on the measure of God's Word in your mouth, and it will determine how long you last in this fight.

Get this, my friend, the measure is nothing more than the capacity to hold the power that you need to get where you're heading. Even greater than that is the understanding that the key is found in the infilling and not in the vessel being used. If I put two vehicles side by side that carried the exact same tank, what would determine the length of miles endured? It wouldn't be the measure of how many gallons are available to the vehicle. It would be determined by the amount of gas that was utilized on the journey. It would be silly to blame the model of the car or even argue that there was somehow an unseen disadvantage between the two. There'd be a logical understanding that one took in more than they gave out, and in turn, it was equipped to reach its destination. After all, just because the capacity is available doesn't mean your fuel gauge isn't showing empty! In the same way, you can be empty, but the infilling of God's Word is what gives you the power to not run out of faith to win!

Friend, stop blaming God for the healing you didn't receive while others received healing. And stop shaking your fist at the cross when you see someone walking in freedom while you are sitting bound to your addiction. Your capacity doesn't hold more than theirs, and theirs doesn't hold more than yours. We've been dealt the same measure and are equally responsible when it comes to filling up on faith!

Just because someone made it further doesn't mean they're more favored. It's a reflection of the responsibility they took, and their actions should encourage you to do the same. Don't allow your spirit to become bitter with anger and resentment. Learn to celebrate with others while taking time to confess, *I am next!*

The words of your mouth will build the faith in your ears. It will fill up the measure and capacity to hold the belief that God can and will in your life! It gives you the power you need to get where you are heading. Utilize what you've been given and stop comparing someone else's gas tank to yours. If it's empty, fill it up!

* * *

Steps Towards Winning

I hope that you are being challenged so far in this process. I want you to remember that this fight is something only YOU can do. No one can make you believe something that you don't want to. And in the same way, no one can throw your fist at the enemy for you. Friend, you must put on your gloves and take the actions necessary to WIN this fight.

One of the first things God told me when I was diagnosed was not to go to Google to confirm or diagnose the diagnosis. Yes, we utilized Google several times already throughout the beginning of the process, but specifically He instructed me to not attach myself to the belief of statistics by searching my diagnosis. This also included unfollowing any breast cancer groups and people who have negative energy, negative beliefs or who contribute to a defeated atmosphere.

Friend, my challenge for you this chapter is to intentionally decide how you fill up your capacity. You can fill up on whatever it is that you choose. But how will you protect your fuel? When I was first diagnosed, I began to join groups of women who we call *breasties* or *pink sisters* in my community. Unfortunately, so many of these groups were full of depression, anxiety and fear.

When I began to share my journey online, I found lots of followers (with good intentions) who shared stories of how their auntie, grandma or cousin passed away with the same diagnosis I had. In a short amount of time I found myself experiencing panic attacks, having nightmares and struggling with my faith.

You know what I had to do? I had to bless them and break the bond. In other words, I knew we had a similar life story and connection, but I had to say goodbye in order to protect my desire to WIN.

Today I want to ask you to do a social media purge. Are you a part of any virtual groups that are listed as "support", but in all reality, they are shackling you to fear? Do you closely follow people with similar stories to yours, and God is asking you to distance yourself because their journey is not your destiny? It's time to look at how you're filling yourself up. We can say all the declarations and scriptures while posting your vision board, but if you're surrounding yourself with voices and stories of others who do not have the same goal in mind as you do, it can sabotage your faith fight.

* * *

Pray it.

Father, I thank You for the ability to take ownership of the capacity I carry. That You have not limited me in any way when it comes to my faith walk, but that I carry the fullness of who You say I am by coming into agreement with what You say I have. Lord, protect my surroundings. Allow me to see with whom I need to link arms with on this journey, and from whom I need to distance myself. Keep me in a state of awareness while I fight with precision and clarity. I speak to every distraction and say that it has to bow its knee. I win because Christ already won! In Jesus' name, Amen.

Chapter 4

Wilderness

Journal

11/23/2020

Hello,

Today is a mile marker. I woke up to golden strands of hair decorating my pillowcase and on the shoulders of my shirt. I'm not sure how I feel about it, but I do know that I'm scared to lose my hair. I don't want to be ugly. I've hid behind my hair all my life, and I'm terrified to not have a place to hide. All day long, I've tossed up the idea of sharing with the world that today is the day my "brave shave" will commence. I feel like the announcement makes it more real, and I'm still not convinced that this should happen.

With every stroke of the brush, golden strands collect. I am currently sitting with my husband this morning, mulling over the idea of continuing to stand in hope that my hair will remain intact, but I think that the both of us know we have been preparing for this day for a while now.

As I sit here, I am presented with a very real opportunity to be overwhelmed with guilt. Has my faith been too shallow to see that my hair remains attached to my head? I'm not sure why God operates the way He does, but I do know that He has a plan; maybe the impact can be greater if the loss is seen?

I refuse to sit in shame when my Savior has set me free from guilt. My faith doesn't determine His faithfulness, but my trust does determine the truth that is experienced in this moment. I believe this experience is not only for me but for many. The weight can be heavy when the world is watching, but I'm learning to lighten it. I do that by recognizing I've not only been created to create, but I serve because I'm being served.

God desires to take care of me. So much so that He's numbered the hairs on my head... or in my case, the number of hairs falling out. I've always thought my job was to serve, create and discover my place, but I'm learning that my job is also to be served, be created and dwell in His place. He is taking care of the work for me. Why have I made it my job? Faith without works is dead, but faith without the One who remains faithful would never exist.

Later...

I have taken a shower, blow-dried and straightened my hair. The number of handfuls is too much for me to ignore. Today I will shave my head at 7pm with the world watching as we worship through the journey. This is not permanent, it's simply the process I must take towards the promise.

I'm nervous, but I am not backing down from what God has declared.

-*Alissa*

It was October 15th, and I was sitting on my back porch when the thought was presented to me. Confused and scared, I made a call to a pastor friends' wife for encouragement. I wasn't lacking support in my life, but I knew her perspective would be covered in grace and not guilt.

I needed a space to widen my view of what Jesus was doing rather than what I saw directly in front of me. Ben and Kim Daily share a huge part of my husband and I's journey, including marrying us at their church, Calvary of Irving. They have a way of presenting life with a beautiful display of freedom and truth, and

Brandon encouraged me to reach out to chat.

With tears streaming down my face, I sat and listened to her voice gently speak grace over my heart. "Alissa, your level of faith is not to convince God of what His Word says. It's to convince you." I questioned her and admitted to the fear that I wouldn't have enough faith to receive healing, and she continued with, "When our faith is small or even nonexistent, He is faithful enough. Do you really think your mustard seed belief is what moves Him? It's His faithfulness that completes it." That's when I heard the Lord speak: *This season I'm taking you through is not about proving yourself to me by serving the Kingdom in order to gain results. It's about My cross serving you so that I can prove I am who I say I am.*

A light bulb went off in my spirit that night. The result of God's Word isn't produced when I conjure something up. It's manifested when I rest in faith the size of a mustard seed knowing God will prove fruit in my life. It's the action of planting myself in belief that allows God to bear the healing. He remains faithful, even when my faith isn't full.

* * *

Write it.

Real quick, you should know the drill, grab a pen or pencil. Before you continue reading this chapter, I want you to brain dump the areas in which you feel your faith isn't full. Once you have been open and honest with yourself, I want you to circle the ones in which you feel you've been striving to prove yourself so that God will answer. Remember, there are no right or wrongs here. This is your story, your faith fight and your journey with Jesus. I'm simply helping you utilize some tools to open your eyes to the truth of His Word. Now, take a minute to do this challenge and we will address it at the end of this chapter.

* * *

There's a common saying that you may have heard a time or two. The Word says that God doesn't give us more than we can bear. Many follow that quote up with a statement like, "There must be a reason you're going through this. If you couldn't handle it, He wouldn't have allowed it." Excuse my bluntness, but how ignorant and non-biblical can we be? Friend, cancer is too much for one person to bear! Divorce is too much for someone to bear! Addiction is too much for an individual to bear! Grief is too heavy for a soul to bear!

How do you think so many people who love Jesus give up frequently and lose their life to suicide? It's because we've been fed a lie that we are equipped to handle life on our own and it leaves us hopeless! Let's dissect this lie together, shall we? The Bible never states that He won't give us more than we can bear. But what does it say exactly?

> "No temptation [regardless of its source] has overtaken or enticed you that is not common to human

experience [nor is any temptation unusual or beyond human resistance]; but God is faithful [to His word—He is compassionate and trustworthy], and He will not let you be tempted beyond your ability [to resist], but along with the temptation He [has in the past and is now and] will [always] provide the way out as well, so that you will be able to endure it [without yielding, and will overcome temptation with joy]."

- 1 Corinthians 10:13, AMP

In other words, temptation beyond your ability is the promise from the Lord! Friend, temptation is ours to bear, not the unbearable! 2 Corinthians 1:9, AMP says, "Indeed, we felt within ourselves that we had received the sentence of death [and were convinced that we would die, but this happened] so that we would not trust in ourselves, but in God who raises the dead." If we were meant to bear the weight of life, then why are we commanded to trust in the Lord and not in ourselves?

Would God contradict Himself by expecting us to bear the burden and asking us to place belief in Him at the same time? He wouldn't! The unbearable was placed on Jesus when He died on the cross! He knew that we could not carry the weight of life in and of ourselves, so He gave us the hope of salvation! Temptation is the burden that we must steward wisely.

1 Corinthians 10:13 goes on to say that He's provided a way out of temptation so that we can endure it without giving up! Well, how do you suppose we do that? Let me share with you a story that I've heard many times before.

One day while sitting on my back porch, the Holy Spirit brought a story back to my mind and gave me a new perspective that changed everything. This is the story of Jesus in the wilderness. Let's read:

> "Now Jesus, full of [and in perfect communication with] the Holy Spirit, returned from the Jordan and was led by the Spirit in the wilderness for forty days, being

tempted by the devil. And He ate nothing during those days, and when they ended, He was hungry. Then the devil said to Him, 'If You are the Son of God, command this stone to turn into bread.' Jesus replied to him, 'It is written and forever remains written, "Man shall not live by bread alone[a]."'

"Then he led Jesus up [to a high mountain] and displayed before Him all the kingdoms of the inhabited earth [and their magnificence] in the twinkling of an eye. And the devil said to Him, 'I will give You all this realm and its glory [its power, its renown]; because it has been handed over to me, and I give it to whomever I wish. Therefore if You worship before me, it will all be Yours.' Jesus replied to him, 'It is written and forever remains written, "You shall worship the Lord your God and serve only Him."'

"Then he led Jesus to Jerusalem and had Him stand on the pinnacle (highest point) of the temple, and said [mockingly] to Him, 'If You are the Son of God, throw Yourself down from here; for it is written and forever remains written, 'He will command His angels concerning You to guard and protect You,' and, 'they will lift You up on their hands, So that You do not strike Your foot against a stone."

"Jesus replied to him, 'It is said [in Scripture], 'you shall not tempt the Lord your God [to prove Himself to you].' When the devil had finished every temptation, he [temporarily] left Him until a more opportune time.

"Then Jesus went back to Galilee in the power of the Spirit, and the news about Him spread through the entire region. And He began teaching in their synagogues and was praised and glorified and honored by all."

- Luke 4:1-14, AMP

At first, I didn't catch what God was trying to show me here. My eyes drifted to the usual aspects of this message, but then I heard Him speak, *How He began is how He won. I never left Him, I led Him.* Then I saw it, verse one was highlighted in a way that I'd never saw before. Full of the Holy Spirit, Jesus was led *by* the Spirit into the wilderness! What? How could that possibly be?

I wonder how many of us are wandering around in our wildernesses, angry at God. We're questioning His faithfulness by asking Him why He's forgotten us. All the while we've never been left, we were being led. Is it possible that your wilderness was intended for you to fulfill His promise in your life? I can't help but challenge your outlook on the current situation because the truth is this: if Jesus can be led into the wilderness, so can you.

I know what you're thinking: *But I didn't want this! This wasn't a part of the plan!* Trust me, I feel you to the depths of my guts on that. If I knew that cancer would be the answer to so many question marks, freedom, breakthroughs and purpose in my life, well, I would have begged God to do it differently. Even Jesus begged God to do it differently. Remember His prayers in the garden before being crucified? Jesus was sweating drops of blood and was greatly troubled in His spirit (Luke 22:44). Yet, He knew this was the plan. Nevertheless, not our will, but His will be done.

The wilderness may not have been something you saw coming, but it was where He has been leading all along. Nothing in your life has taken Him by surprise. It could have been out of your control or an attack from the enemy. Maybe some things were due to choices you've made. Regardless, He knew your story and assigned a way out before you ever concocted a plan to begin with. Jesus' wilderness led Him to purpose and so can yours.

You know who else was led into the wilderness? The Israelites. After being delivered out of slavery, abuse and watching their people get murdered daily, God intervened. He came with the Word of a promised land, but led them into the wilderness to get them there. It was a journey that should have taken eleven days to complete. Instead, they circled around for forty years because of their unbelief. The entire time they complained and were disobedient. What's interesting to me is that they lived out daily miracles and still marched around in circles. Food was provided from Heaven, fire led them by night and clouds by day. They were engulfed in the supernatural and still refused to get their mindsets right.

This taught me that it's possible to see God show up over and over again, and *still* struggle with receiving your promise. Let this remind you, your mindset and mouth will absolutely keep you repeating cycles in your life if you're not careful! So, how do we break away from these strongholds?

Let me ask you this: to break a cycle in the natural, what must take place? The physical is often a picture of the spiritual, and it will open your understanding in new ways if you let it. Naturally, women were created to repeat cycles monthly, and physically a seed must be planted for the cycle to be broken and for new life to spring forth. Catch this, if you're tired of marching around in the wilderness, if everything looks dried up and dead, then you must break the cycle by understanding the seed of faith!

What seeds are you planting, friend? I can't write this enough; what you say, you sow, and it will reap a harvest in your life! Someone said it this way: "If you don't like what you're seeing, you must change what you're saying!" The wilderness in our life is repeated when our words aren't renewed. If the Israelites' mouths can keep them from their promise, then yours isn't any different! Sow the seed that you want to see produced!

One story shows a cycle while the other shows celebration! Let's go back to Luke 4 where Jesus was led into His wilderness. How was His story different? When we read over this passage, we saw that there was a whole lot of saying and replying taking place. The enemy said, and Jesus replied with *It is written*.

So far, we've talked a lot about how the enemy approaches us in the fight of faith. By painting pictures of defeat and fear, he waits for our response. His approach in this scenario is no different. Let me encourage you, any time the Spirit leads you, He also equips you to win.

The beautiful thing about this passage is that Jesus didn't respond with anything outside of the Word that we were provided with. Everything that was spoken was written in the Word. In other words, your wilderness responds to the Word in your mouth. It wasn't that He had some magical formula or some heavenly wisdom that we couldn't tap into ourselves. No, He did what *we* can do! He gave us an example of how to overcome the temptation of which 1 Corinthians 10:13 spoke.

Does this make more sense now? You will not be tempted beyond your ability because Jesus showed us how to win over temptation! He was led into the wilderness specifically to be tempted, and He broke the lie of cycles by planting seeds of faith. With the Word in His mouth, He sowed promise into His life. He wasn't swayed by what He saw or felt, but stood firmly on the truth that was written.

From there, the enemy left, and the last verse says, "Then Jesus went back to Galilee in the power of the Spirit."

Friend, is it possible that you've been led to confront the enemy so that you can return with power? Your wilderness is the answer to your winning! Instead of getting angry at God, ask Him what cycles in your life need to be broken.

You were assigned to this wilderness to take hold of the promised land! The only way you are going to lay your hands on victory is by confronting the enemy. How are you doing with this? What are you speaking during the journey? Are you murmuring and complaining, or are you replying with, *It is written*?

In order to leave with power, you must be led by the pursuit of what God says about you. Let me ask you: what good is it to be led by the Spirit, if you don't leave full of power to win your fight? When Jesus left the wilderness, that chapter goes on to say that He taught, healed the sick and casted out demons. Stop despising this season you're in! It's preparation for the purpose He has for your life!

Sometimes God takes us through seasons of confrontation in order to sever the cycles that keep manifesting in our lives. Truth is, if He took you to the promise before you were ready, you'd lose by default. If He gave you a win before you knew how to steward the victory, you'd march right back into defeat.

This fight is not because you've been *left*. It's because you're being *led*. The promised land is waiting, but the length of time it takes you to get there depends on your willingness to believe. Open your mouth and sow seeds that will produce the harvest for which you are believing in God.

It was a game changer when I realized the cross came to serve me when life was unbearable. Christ never meant for me to prove myself; He came to prove His Word. He knew that I would fail every time and gave me a way out by finishing the work for me. My husband says it this way, "Christ died my death, so I can live His life."

He covered me with grace by placing within me the ability to operate in faith. The greatest revelation that you could ever perceive is the fullness of salvation provided on the cross. The same cross that came to save, is the same cross that came to heal, deliver, provide and restore. It brings freedom and equips you with authority. It removes condemnation and replaces it with the Holy Spirit. It leads you during dry desert places and empowers you to gather the harvest. That's the truth about God's faithfulness. He never left. He always leads. He's proving Himself to you and joining you in the midst.

Remember the story of Jesus sleeping in the boat (Matthew 8:23-27)? Suddenly a furious storm appeared on the lake. The Word says that waves swept over the boat and that the disciples were terrified of drowning. Were they alone? No, Jesus joined them in the midst of chaos and spoke peace over the violence of the sea.

What about the passage that talks about three friends, Shadrach, Meshach, and Abednego (Daniel 3:16-28)? They refused to bow down to any other God and were thrown into a fiery furnace. In fact, Nebuchadnezzar was so angry they wouldn't worship his idol that he commanded them to turn the furnace that they were thrown in seven times hotter. The flames were so hot that the men who threw them in were killed immediately! Still, they said this, "Did we not cast three men into the fire? I see four men loose, walking in the midst, and they have no hurt; and the form of the fourth is like the Son of God" (v25).

Jesus doesn't leave us in the hell and storms of our life. He joins us in the midst every single time.

Friend, He's proving Himself to you in the wilderness. He's equipped you to overcome the temptation to quit and give up! He's empowered you with words that are alive and carry weight. He's not asking you to do something that Jesus hasn't already done.

Your faith is not to convince God that He should do it, it's to convince you that it's already done. When you finally stop begging Him to do the thing He finished in the spiritual and replace it with the belief that it is indeed finished, *everything* will change. His Word in your mouth allows the wilderness to produce the fruit of promise in your life. Stop asking Him to work it out and start thanking Him for the finished work on the cross!

* * *

Steps Towards Winning

Remember that paper of "proving points" we circled? Get it out and read over it. How do these areas make you feel? Are you discouraged with them? Do you feel like your faith is failing you in these areas? Do you feel tired when you think of overcoming them? Take a moment and write your thoughts down before picking this book back up.

Okay friend, let me repeat myself, your faith is not to convince God that He should do it, it's to convince you that it's already done. I had you write these areas down and sort through your thought process so that you'd be aware of *the fists* that are being thrown in that direction.

When a boxer is preparing for a fight, they study the opponent's strengths and weaknesses. This is what we are doing here. We're learning to see where we are weak so that God can be strong. When our faith isn't full in one area, we can trust that He is faithful. First, we have to recognize the weakness so that we can strengthen our belief system in that area. Now that we recognize them, let's speak over them.

* * *

Pray it.

Father, I thank You for Your faithfulness. I recognize the areas that don't feel full in my life, and I surrender them to You. I shift my perspective when it comes to proving myself, and I ask that You help me understand that the power is in the belief that it's done and not in the pressure of begging You to do it. I speak to the situation now and say that it is finished. Not because I'm perfect. Not because I'm worthy. But because Christ already paid the price when He stretched His arms out wide for me on the cross. I win because He won. In Jesus' name, Amen.

Chapter 5

Strike the Lion

Journal

11/24/2020

Hello,

I'm sitting here with a buzzed head at my second chemo treatment. Although it only took me two weeks to lose my hair, I'm killing the game if I do say so myself.

My honey is the best and brought me breakfast from Sonic. He's been special delivering food and coffee to me. I think it's his way of taking care of me since no one can come back to the infusion room with me. It's hard being in here alone due to Covid, but he makes it easier when I get to sit by the window seat. He parks right outside of the window so that we can Facetime and still see each other.

The process this morning was very easygoing. With a quick bee sting to my chest, they accessed my port, took my blood, gave me my meds and began my infusion with Adriamycin (one of three chemotherapies I'll be partaking in over the next six months). This one is bright red and has earned the nickname "red devil" in the cancer community. I personally like to say what my husband has said, "Alissa, the red devil is being introduced to the blood of Jesus once it enters your body."

Today was also time for my second Zoladex shot which keeps me in menopause throughout this journey. Bran and I are still standing on the promise of God for children, and this will help protect my eggs from treatment. It also stops the estrogen production since the tumor was positive for hormonal growth. Although the shot is done with a 14-gauge needle, I once again didn't feel a thing! That's something I've been specifically targeting in prayer. The way Jesus allows me to go through this process while protecting me from physical torture is absolutely a testament to the fact that miracles are real.

Last night was one for the books. I shaved my head, and it was surprisingly freeing. The fear was not found in losing my hair, it was found in losing my identity. It was wrapped up in my inability to hide and expose my insecurities. It was allowing me to be placed in a very vulnerable position while being terrified of the exposure. To boil it down, the fear was in becoming uncaged.

I've never been very confident in my looks. In fact, I've always been unsure of my physical appearance and what I have to offer as a woman. Be it because of my experience with rape, the porn addiction found in every guy I loved before Bran, divorce or the mean girls at school... the truth is this area has paralyzed me for most of my life. Without hair in which to find confidence and a hiding place to retreat, I wasn't sure how I'd cope with my life. Yet, here I am- proudly sitting with my leopard print turban and rocking my new buzzed look as I'm surrounded by the balding 60 -80-year-old cancer patients this morning.

The truth is, freedom overwhelmed me last night. I believe decades of chains fell off as locks of hair hit the floor, and while every strand of security was being stripped from my head, I felt secure in the One who was strengthening me in that moment. Brandon, our girls, my in-loves and my dear friend, Candi, gathered around me as I pushed the "live" button on Facebook for the world to join me.

We were all brave together as my "brave shave" commenced. We cried, laughed, joked and experienced very sobering moments of love. My husband and kids took turns cutting my hair and shaving my head as thousands of people sent beautiful comments of love and encouragement throughout the process.

I've never felt more exposed and more accepted than I did at that moment. I'll remember it forever. There was a point where my oldest daughter tried to hand me the mirror to reveal my new look. I broke down sobbing in fear as everyone watched. I was too scared to look at myself because that meant I'd finally see the girl that's been hiding her whole life. I didn't know what she'd look like. I didn't know if I could accept her, and I was afraid to confront her because she's been trying to break free for decades.

And I'd kept her caged.

Unable to control my tears on the live feed, thousands of eyes watched as I fought internally with unlocking the cage I've lived in for most of my life. Those bars of insecurity had haunted me. The iron behind the fear that locked me away had become so familiar. With limited space to exercise my authority or for my voice to be heard, I accepted my cage as "enough" and found myself tamed to the comfort of my own confinement.

I've learned that strength isn't only developed, it's discovered. And this was one of those moments where I felt the discovery of strength, even in my weakness. Once we got to the end of my hair transformation, my husband and I had a moment of true empathy. As he cleaned up the buzz cut that I never knew I'd wear, I looked up at a man who was trying so desperately to hold it together for the sake of my heart. When our eyes locked, we both felt every emotion of this process hitting us straight in the gut. We embraced each other and wept violently. From the depths of our spirits, we grieved together while an audience of people felt the strength, love and pain. They all looked upon the process of what it meant to trust God in the midst of hardship.

Afterwards, I allowed myself to truly look in the mirror and embrace the woman uncaged. She was beautiful. She was strong. She knew she was there all along. With a leopard turban to represent the roar that had just been released, I took my crew inside to celebrate the faithfulness of God as we worshiped through the storm together. B and I have done lots of live worship sessions before, but there was something extra special about this one. Freedom in my spirit leapt, even through my grief. This was the moment I experienced the joy of the Lord in a way that overwhelmed the thing trying to overwhelm me.

There was a holy presence in the house as we worshiped through the hardest moment we'd experienced as a family. Jesus was there, and everyone felt it. When we pushed "end" on our live, and all the eyes were off us, I collapsed in my husband's arms. My friend captured a picture that I'll forever cherish of that moment. We sat in that space, embracing each other as we simultaneously took deep breaths of pain, relief, grief, peace and freedom. Grace overwhelmed us there. Through adversity, we rested in the certainty that His promise still stands. He never fails, and He wouldn't stop now. That was the beginning of the promise.

Once we were done tearing down our worship gear, I went to the bathroom to take in my new look, and that's the moment that I saw it. I was no longer overcome with sorrow. I was overcome with freedom. There was something so heroic about looking fear in the face while raising my hands and releasing a voice of triumph. It was the space where violence tried to overcome my story, but victory overruled it.

Something broke.

Something shattered.

Something fell victim to the sound of my praise.

And it wasn't me. It was cancer, insecurity, comparison, lack of confidence, tragedy, weakness, pain, regret and so much more. Freedom overcame the facts of life. I've learned that it's possible to be in the middle of an impossible situation and not be the one to break. Instead, I'd broken forth... I'd uncaged myself. Now it was time to reign & roar.

-Alissa

There's a memory that will ever live rent-free in my brain. I was twenty-three years young, lugging around a two and one-year old. It was Kinsleigh and

Aurora's first trip to the zoo, and I do believe that I was more excited than either of them that day. Some of my favorite memories as a kid were hot summer afternoons spent with my cousins, exploring the animal exhibits. I'd often wonder what it'd be like when I was grown and could take kids of my own on adventures like those. I was determined to breathe in every moment of that day and made it my mission to come prepared. With a quick photo shoot by the entrance sign, I loaded up the stroller, handed them sippy cups, slapped on their hats and kept my phone handy to take all the necessary videos.

One by one, I intently studied the look on my girls' faces as I introduced them to our new furry friends. There wasn't much excitement most of the time. In fact, I wrestled with the stroller, snacks and hats more than anything else. Despite the chaos of being a young mom of two in the middle of an animal kingdom, something caught my eye and stuck with me in such a way that I've pondered it for years. It wasn't the peacocks that captivated my babies with their bright colorful dances. The monkeys didn't in trance them with their swinging acrobats from one tree to the next. Not even the elephant in all its "gentle giant" vibes could keep their attention fixed. No, it wasn't until we circled around the exhibit that the attention of every person in the room was demanded, and the girls became hypnotized like the rest of us. Can you guess what animal it was?

Yes, the king himself was the only animal my girls cared about that day. Mr. Lion even became a stuffed souvenir my two-year-old named Leo and still has today (twelve years later). My point is there's something about a lion that completely enthralls human beings. Maybe it's the beauty they so effortlessly carry. Or it could be the fear and respect simultaneously drawn out of every living thing in their presence. Regardless, I've found there's some things to be learned from the king of the jungle, and I've carried them with me through the tough seasons of life, cancer being one.

It had only been thirteen days since I encountered the "red devil", and my nearly two-week gift was waking to platinum hair lining my pillowcase. Although I prepared my mind for this moment, I didn't think it'd come so soon. With a strand of hope left, I decided to wash and style what remained to see just how much time we could hang on to my depleted tresses. It didn't take long for me to realize the loss was inevitable as clumps of hair fell onto the bathroom counter effortlessly.

Throughout my journey, I vlogged all the moments in hopes to show others what faith looks like in the midst of the fight. There were times of strength and other times of sorrow, but this was a raw moment as I watched my identity transform completely in front of me.[3]

From the moment my oncologist mentioned the words *losing your hair*, I decided to order some turbans on Amazon. The first one I purchased had a leopard print pattern and I immediately knew this would be what I'd wear for my brave shave party. *I am woman/ Hear me*

[3] You can find the videos on my YouTube channel here-
https://www.youtube.com/@thealissaholt

roar rose in my spirit as my mind flashed back to the 22-year-old girl standing in front of Mr. Lion with her daughters. She had her own beasts to fight at the time, and here she was nine years later, but this beast came to take her life.

I could almost hear the dirty Philistine threatening to feed my body to cancer by burying me in defeat, and can I tell you, the opportunity to submit was very real. When evening came, I found myself standing in front of the bathroom mirror at my mother-in-law's home. I gazed at my hair while pointing my finger at my reflection, "You will not die. You are not defeated. You will open your mouth and declare the Word of the Lord. Alissa, you win."

After my little pep talk, my family and I gathered on the deck outside and pushed live on our Facebook feed. My husband and children took turns buzzing the blonde off my once healthy head and our tears were felt through the screen. Losing my hair that night felt much like being placed on exhibit. Thousands watched in awe as they tried to grasp the courage being displayed despite the cancer. A leopard print turban and a night of worship would become the beginning of uncaging the lion within my heart. It was at that moment that weakness became the breeding ground for strength to be known in my journey.

Friend, one of the biggest misconceptions when it comes to a fight of faith is that we must outlast the beast in order to win. Throughout this journey, I've found that this couldn't be further from the truth. I don't have to outlast the beast; he is the one that must attempt to outlast me.

I'm reminded of a story from my Bible college days that struck the lion within me. One of my professors at Rhema shared a time in his life when he lived in California while managing an acting career. He was speaking about the authority and power we carry without even realizing it and explained an encounter he had with a witch on the street.

While walking one day and minding his own business, he heard a voice yell out, "You're a Christian, aren't you?"

Startled, he looked around and studied his clothes to see if he wore something that identified him as a pastor. Realizing he was in normal street clothes, he asked, "Who, me?"

The witch didn't waste time and responded, "Yes, you! You don't realize who you are, do you? You Christians walk around here weak and uneasy about your identity, but if you could only see into the spiritual realm like we do, then you'd know better." He obviously wanted to know more so he began to ask her what exactly she meant.

She continued by saying, "I'm a witch and interact with demons every day. My gift is seeing into the spiritual realm, and I am continuously amazed at how stupid you Christians are. I can spot you from a mile away. You all have a bright glow that surrounds you and puts out any realm of darkness you encounter. Demonic forces are literally scared of you. I watch them physically tremble in your presence, yet you Christians are terrified of them! If you only knew the power you carry, you'd never be scared of demons a day in your life. None of you know who you are, and it makes us laugh."

Friend, to win, there are two things that must be understood before going into battle. The first thing is to have a clear understanding of your name as a child of God, and the second thing is to recognize your authority through Jesus. It's no surprise that lions often signify strength, courage and power. They are identified as *king* because of their raw ability to dominate their habitat, and they do so without fear of their adversaries.

It's funny to me how much power we give the beasts in our life when we carry The King with us every day. How can we lose when He has already won the battle? So many of us fail because we have focused on the appearance of what we are fighting, not realizing it's an illusion.

"Your enemy the devil prowls around like a lion looking for someone to devour."

-   1 Peter 5:8, TPT

Many would read this scripture and focus on the beast, but I want to challenge you to shift your focus to the lie found within the context of the scripture. Peter is not saying the enemy is powerful, strong and able. He is simply saying that the enemy is like a lion who's merely looking for prey. *What does that mean, Alissa?* It means there's only one king and His name is Jesus.

The reason we feel devoured by the beast is because we've accepted a false pretense that this thing is too big for our God. Remember, David stood before Goliath and immediately told him how big his Creator was despite what he saw. Likewise, when physical reality tried to shake my faith, I stood in the mirror and declared my future.

It may feel like your situation appears to be more than a view right now. It may have woven its way into your story by becoming a tangible reality in your life. But read my words, friend: this is where faith must rise and strike the lion within your heart.

Despite what religion has taught you, your destination is not to fight a good fight of faith the rest of your life without seeing results. It's to have the faith to fight, knowing Jesus already won the war! Newsflash, counterfeit lions have no power over the King. They may roar loud, but they don't reign over the destiny God has for your life. The key is learning how to unlock the cage we've been trying to live in while believing in the power we need to overcome.

When I stood at the exhibit with my girls, I recognized the powerful potential living behind bars, and nine years later, I discovered the purpose inside of me needed uncaging as well. Cancer might have been a beast, but the real power was found in my belief that God was greater.

* * *

Write it.

This challenge comes with a collection of questions. What in your life has tried to behave like a lion? How has it lied to you with its roars through your suffering? What has it allowed you to believe about your God?

It's time to strike the lion and discover the name and power that you carry. Friend, grab your journal and take a moment to write it out. You will not understand the power you carry unless you discover the power that these circumstances have held over your life. For faith to become tangible, fear must lose its grip. Take as long as you need to have an open and honest conversation with Jesus, and then pick this book back up when you're finished.

* * *

When you realize that the King is on your side, you'll find that the characteristics of lions can be very empowering. For instance, their eyes are six times more sensitive to light compared to the human eye. This allows their night vision to be far better than their prey and gives them the ability to be the hunter rather than the hunted. I wonder how many times we live life from a *I'm being hunted* mindset? So often our life is followed by cute little sayings that we nonchalantly say without any second thought. "When it rains, it pours" is something we joke about, or "I can't win for losing" is an expression we carelessly toss around.

By casually coming into agreement with these seemingly innocent phrases, we find ourselves in a tug of war with the idea of struggle versus victory. Our inability to see in the night hour traps us with fear and completely disables our faith. Friend, to win, our vision cannot be fixed on the darkness around us. It must be focused on the light within us.

When I shifted my perspective from fear to faith, I was able to utilize the authority of Christ rather than grasping for the ability to survive on my own. You may not have the capability to see what's taking place in the darkness right now, but you do have the authority to allow the light that lives within you to guide you through the valley. The shadow may be casting a very real giant over your life, but remember one thing, shadows are nothing more than illusions.

They disguise themselves like lions and we tend to fall for it every time. Remember, shadows make the tiniest things look huge. Think about this, there wouldn't even be a shadow if light weren't present in the first place! I had to see who Jesus was in the cancer before I could find the answers that were staring me in the face all along.

Stop looking at the illusion as if God is absent, and recognize His presence is closer than you realize!

"Even though I walk through the [sunless] valley of the shadow of death, I fear no evil, for You are with me; Your rod [to protect] and Your staff [to guide], they comfort and console me."

- Psalms 23:4, AMP

When I was in my valley season, I had to make a decision to fix my voice on the truth of His Word by making no exceptions in what I said. There were many opportunities for me to get discouraged and become overwhelmed with doubt, but I had to see the shadow for what it was rather than what it was trying to become in my life. I did this by taking drastic measures.

Many would look at me cross-eyed and call me charismatic with my approach, but the truth is, God's Word is not logical! It's radical! We must stop watering down the power it carries by filtering it with pitiful stories about our circumstance. If God said it, I believe it, and that settles it!

When talking about my journey, many would innocently say, "Alissa has breast cancer" or "We're believing her cancer is going to be healed". It didn't take me but a split second to boldly correct friends and family stating, "It's not mine! I am healed!" One lady even made me a shirt that said: *My God is bigger than my cancer.* Out of faith, I refused to wear it. In fact, I threw it away! I understood that every time I stated that it was mine, I was agreeing with the diagnosis over the decree that God said healing was provided on the cross! I refused to give power to the shadow and made a conscious decision to give authority to the light of God's Word instead.

You may be walking through the shadow right now, but the only way to see through the darkness is by utilizing the light of hope inside you. What does He say about your situation? How are you assessing it? You'll never know what you have if you don't know what He says!

So many times, we are fighting blind when He's provided us with a whole book of decrees to utilize. Let me help you out, if it's written, then it's meant to be spoken. Look at 1 John 1:5, AMP with me, "This is the message [of God's promised revelation] which we have heard from Him and now announce to you, that God is Light [He is holy, His message is truthful, He is perfect in righteousness], and in Him there is no darkness at all [no sin, no wickedness, no imperfection]."

When light is exposed, darkness is diminished every single time. But how do we expose darkness? It's simple, but we make it hard. Light is released when you loose your mouth!

There's a story that I heard from Mark Hankins about the power of sound that's stuck with me for years. He was sitting on an airplane when he picked up a 1994 Time Magazine article titled, *What's Hiding in the Quarks?* It talked about a new model for an atom called the nucleus, and how in years prior, they studied the function of protons, neutrons and electrons.

While they began to dissect this theory more, they realized there was another component inside the atom called a quark. Delving further into that, they found something smaller hidden within the quark itself! Many didn't know what to call it, so they labeled it the *God particle*. Others said we're just looking at a sound wave and concluded that the smallest building block of all matter is sound itself.

"In the beginning God created the heavens and the earth.. And God said, 'Let there be light'; and there was light."

- Genesis 1:1,3, AMP

Friend, sound is what scientifically holds everything together! If the beginning started with a sound that produced light, then your sound must release before you can see in the darkness! Every word spoken from God is wrapped in power to ignite the darkest valley with hope! Remember, fearing evil is impossible when your vision is full of faith. So how do we get to a place where fear does not move us even when the valley is scary? We open our ears to hear! Faith can only come through hearing what God says (Romans 10:17), but you can't hear it unless you speak it! In other words, how you steward what you're speaking will determine the vision you carry to get out of that pit!

Don't forget, lions have great night vision because their eyes are six times more sensitive to light. When we become more sensitive to the light of God's Word, we will have the ability to see clearly in impossible situations.

Here's the problem, we say that we see what God says, but we live based on what our physical eye is telling us. Friend, you can't see what God says when you're focused on what your life is saying. Seeing is believing and saying is agreeing. What are your eyes focused on most of the time? I promise your vision is shaping your belief system. If you don't like what you see, you'll have to change what you say. Stop agreeing with the circumstance in front of you by putting your sight on the shadow rather than the Savior!

Friend, when we tap into the authority of who Christ is inside of us by speaking the Word, we begin to practice our roar rather than panic and run, which leads me to my next characteristic of the lion inside of you. Did you know that these beasts mostly roar at night and can be heard up to five miles away? If that isn't power, then I don't know what is! In other words, silent roars do not command authority, and decrees are mostly heard in the darkness. You must stop allowing the enemy to steal your voice by locking your tongue down to a victim mentality! You'll know that your faith is activated when your sound agrees with what God says despite what you see. It's the Word of God in your mouth that causes demons to tremble from miles away.

It's so easy to become a victim to your valley, but the valley needs to hear your voice! Do not allow yourself to identify with the panic of the situation rather than the power that's inside of you! Cancer would have been easy for me to submit to. I carried a diagnosis, bald head and housed a port in my chest so chemo could consume me on a weekly basis. My outside appearance screamed cancer in every way possible. Looking with my physical eyes, it would only seem logical to victimize myself to disease. But seeing with my spiritual eyes, I recognized the truth of healing. I may have been in the pit, but there was power in the roar of my tongue.

Silence cannot command anything. It's the shout of victory despite the valley that activates faith. It creates vision for you to see where God is taking you even when it looks hopeless.

The more I spoke, the more I saw. The louder I declared, the stronger I got. It didn't happen overnight, and it was not for the faint of heart. I had to remain consistent even when I felt like quitting. Three times a day, my alarm would ring, and I'd stand to my feet as an act of faith. Three times a day, I'd drag myself to the bathroom mirror, weak, bald and scarred. Three times a day, I'd look myself in the eyeball sockets and declare the Word of life over the reflection of death staring back at me. My roar was practiced in the night hour of my life, not when things looked good. My sight was strengthened in the darkness, not when I could see the end result. It was my sound that determined what I saw about my fight.

Friend, it's time for you to strike the lion inside of you and get up from this valley! Your voice is waiting to be heard, and your vision is waiting to be released. Only you can make the choice.

* * *

Steps Towards Winning

This is where the rubber meets the road, my friend. You've taken time to write scripture, make declarations and create vision boards. I've challenged you to recognize your counterfeit beast and to lose your grip on fear. But where do we go from here?

Notice, lion's eyes have greater vision in the night and their voices are more heard in the darkness. I wonder if that's your reality today. Is the depth of your valley demanding a fight within you or is it paralyzing you with fear? When I was in my valley, the Lord told me that it must hear my voice. For a chemo patient, that is difficult. In fact, there were many days when I had no voice. I would become so weak that my head felt like a 50-pound weight, and my breath struggled to find space in my lungs. Still, my alarm would ring, and my body would physically fight to do what faith was requiring from me.

I remember rolling my dead weight over in bed as my hands trembled to find my collection of scriptures. I pushed off my pillow and felt as though my 31-year-old body had become a 90-year-old lady. My girls would carry me to the bathroom so that I could look myself in the eyes as I declared life over my situation, and my husband would beg me to let him help. "Liss, please," with tears staining his cheeks, "Just lay there. Let me read these words over you. Please, just rest. Let your body heal. I can help you with this love." My response was always the same, "No, my valley must hear my voice. My mountain can't move off of your mouth. It's my faith that I must speak."

Here's your step; are you ready? What action is the Lord asking you to make today? For me, it was a physical movement towards healing while voicing my faith. If I was believing that I was healed, I had to act like I was healed. Maybe yours is a dietary change as you partner with God in healing. It could be a sacrifice in friendships that are no longer useful for the space in which God is taking you. Or possibly He is asking you to lay down desires and pick up new dreams. Take some time to pray over your night hour and ask the Father how you can fight with action.

* * *

Pray it.

Father, I thank You for guidance and empowerment; that You've never placed expectation on me to fight this battle on my own, but that You've promised to be with me every step of the way. I'm asking You for active steps; that the clarity for what it is I'm to do in this waiting season would be clear. That You would help me say yes to the challenge at hand, and that You would equip me with the answers I need. I speak to the valley and say that I WIN in darkness. My voice will carry and my faith will be strong. I see exactly where I'm headed because the Holy Spirit in me knows the final destination. In Jesus' name, Amen.

Chapter 6
Led Faith

Journal
Spoken Word

3-10-21

153 days.

20 weeks.

12 rounds of poison.

5 months of menopause.

And a 31-year-old woman.

A once healthy body morphed into a zombie,

Craving the taste of life as tears fall calmly from

A beautiful shade of green.

Begging to see black.

Legs desperate for the sleep that stillness makes them lack.

The taste of paper, traded for the flavor on her tongue.

Muscles throb for peace and beg for mercy, just for once.

Tell me, how can you run towards healing when you can barely feel your toes?

How can you fight in faith when this is not something that you chose?

Sleep that's not had.

Energy gone bad.

Dreams that aren't imagined.

One step at a time.

One breath at a time.

'Cause life as you knew, it's been abandoned.

Yet I still feel that hope, beating in my chest.

The breath of life still comes to breathe into all that's been called dead,

And I don't know how it works because it still remains unseen.

It's evidence despite the things that come from a disease.

———-----------

It says I have called your name before sickness ever had one.

I wrote the plan I had for you before illness ever happened.

I didn't change My mind,

And this doesn't change the cross.

Your present suffering will not bring forth loss.

Nothing broken,

Nothing missing.

Nothing will be wasted.

I saw it from the moment that your life had been created.

Didn't take Me by surprise

'Cause I said that it is finished.

This thing can't take your life

Unless you let it steal your image...

'In the image & the likeness of God, you were created.'

Identity is where your faith is truly activated.

If you know who you are, then disease can't steal your name.

Your destiny was set in place before this diagnosis was a thing.

So, the question isn't how- the question is in who.

Not who I am 'cause that don't change,

The question is:

Who are you?

What do you believe 'cause of the battles in your mind?

—-----------

We fight against reality and what He says is mine.

The power's in the choice to agree with what we see.

Whether that is found in flesh

Or faith in the unseen.

What you believe is what you'll see and that's what you will have.

Agreement with the thing you see is what brings it all to pass.

So, if disease defines you, then healing will be missed.

Not because it wasn't yours,

But true identity was dismissed.

You didn't see your image reflecting your Creator.

You saw your diagnosis as your only life's dictator.

So yes, cancer is a thing...

but Jesus is the Healer...

And death? It holds no sting.

'Cause His Word is even greater.

I'll activate the Word by declaring that I'm freed.

Delivered from death's door and choosing to believe.

I will live and I won't die.

I declare it every day.

Even when I feel like death is felt in every way.

I know that this is hard,

But it is not the end.

Disease of any kind was met before it all began.

So, repeat after me:

I am healed

and I am whole.

Nothing broken, nothing missing,

My mind, I will control.

He said it on the cross,

"It is done."

I can overcome this disease

'Cause Jesus already won.

-Alissa

It was my twelfth round of chemotherapy when I felt it. Twenty weeks in and my body was begging for mercy. There were permanent weights attached to my eyelids and unbearable pain was surging through my bones. Simple tasks felt like strength training, and suddenly the bright, motivated and talented woman I once knew, no longer existed. She was gone and I was grieving the life that she lost. The night after round twelve was unforgettable. After taking my medications, I drifted off into a world searching for no pain.

The only problem was, I could feel my body dying. Laying in a bed of poison, the breath in my chest began to slow as the depth of air became shallower by the minute. I felt my lungs gasping for air as I continued to sleep in a haze of subconscious awareness. That's when I felt my spirit try to leave my body. As I began floating upward, I felt my chest remain still.

No breath was entering or leaving when I heard a voice clearly speak, *You will live and not die. You will declare My works. Alissa, by faith, lead yourself into lasting promise.* My eyes jerked open as I gasped for air. Clutching my chest, I sat up in bed with panic to breathe.

My husband jarred himself awake at the sound of my desperation and frantically asked me what was wrong. "I was dying. I could feel myself dying. But a voice woke me up saying, 'I'll live.'"

There was only one other time I felt this during my journey. It was very similar in circumstance but rather than hearing the voice of peace, I heard the voice of destruction. *I will kill you! You WILL die and I'll steal your future!* It woke me up in fear, as anxiety filled my room and I was spiritually very aware of the warfare going on. It went much deeper than physical misfortune. This was a demonic attack and it was trying to kill the destiny in my life.

When I woke to the words, *By faith, lead yourself into lasting promise,* I took time to ask the Lord what He meant. I think it's so important to never assume anything when it comes to our relationship with Christ, but to become students of His Word as we listen for His voice. I sat with this experience for days before He really began to speak. What I heard would take my faith walk to another level of responsibility. It would dismantle the belief that I need someone to assist me and would teach me that I am enough to lead myself.

When you truly think about it, you'll see that so many areas of our lives spiritually have been led by pastors, leaders and spiritual voices of authority. For you, it could have been your parents, grandma or your favorite Sunday school teacher. Regardless, you were led from the moment that you met Jesus.

If it weren't for the opportunity to be led in a salvation prayer, you would have never confessed Christ as your personal Savior. If you weren't led into that worship moment, you might have never encountered freedom from the thing that kept you stuck in defeat. Maybe it was an altar call that led you to respond to the grace of God. Whatever it was, we are used to being led, but are we accustomed to leading?

What I found during this space of acknowledgment was this: led faith is not lasting faith. It isn't until you learn to lead yourself in faith that you begin to acquire lasting results. Hear me out, there is a time and place for every season of our life as Christians. Thank the Lord for the moments of partnership when it comes to someone else agreeing, believing and standing in the gap with us. I know for sure that I needed those moments desperately throughout my life, and I'm forever grateful for the ones who didn't give up on me. They taught me endurance and they played a huge role in my yes to Jesus.

The problem is, if you are waiting to be led, you'll also wait for someone to fight on your behalf. Friend, winners don't rely on an outside source to do their dirty work. It's only when you enter the cage, independent of anyone else, that the bell can ring and the fight can start. Your coach is always on the sidelines, but you are the one swinging fists.

It's silly to expect the guy who's screaming at you from the ropes to produce the knockout punch needed to win. He's not the one standing in the cage! You are! Therefore, you must be willing to do the work to get the job done. Do we listen to the voice of wisdom guiding us during the fight?

Yes! Do we wait for him to step in and do the job for us? No! Your fight only gets lasting results when you start to lead yourself in a win. Thank God for the training that it takes to get us to the cage, but the match is solely dependent on you stepping out and leading yourself into victory. There's strength stewarded in the training, but there's power utilized in the fight!

Let me say it again, *led* faith can only get you so far in this journey. I found that the prayers prayed, calls made and social media posts supporting me in love were all very comforting, but they weren't completing the work for me. I had to step out on my own. I had to understand that the final swing must be swung from my own fists, not from *their* faith. I knew that the healing received was not going to come from the prayers of hundreds but my posture of hope.

My favorite scripture during my battle with the pink monster is found in Hebrews 10:23, TPT, "So now wrap your heart tightly around the hope that lives within us, knowing that God always keeps his promises!" What is hope, Alissa? Well, the very next chapter in Hebrews tells us that it's the reality of faith! Hebrews 11:1, NLT says, "Faith shows the reality of what we hope for; it is the evidence of things we cannot see."

I want to be clear before we move on. Do I believe in the prayers of others? Yes, the Word is very clear where two or more are gathered together, and agree concerning anything, then He will do it (Matthew 18:20). It also says that if you are sick, you should be brought before the elders of the church and be prayed over for healing (James 5:14). There are many verses that discuss the gathering together of believers and how your prayers can empower the church.

I believe that those prayers are to cover, uplift and strengthen us! It is to give us the ability to stand when things are falling to pieces. It allows us to regain our composure so that we can finish the work being done. Led faith is great strength training for your spirit! It builds you up and sharpens your belief system. But lasting faith is when you operate in the power to receive the thing you're fighting for. It's when you tap into a *your faith has made you whole* (Mark 5:34) moment that everything changes. So yes, pray with others and agree in faith! But understand, the prayer of agreement is to cover you in grace enough to RECEIVE, not for someone else to receive it for you!

When I was believing for healing, no one led me to write scripture down. No one advised me to post it on my mirrors or carry it in my purse. There were no coaching sessions where someone taught me how to create a vision board of faith for my spirit to take hope in. I had to become the leader of my own winning fight. I had to learn to trust the Holy Spirit inside of me as I obeyed the guidelines He placed before me. It took work! It required discipline! It dismantled the ability to lean on others for manifestation and put the responsibility on my belief in the cross! Take a look at this,

> "Then they came to Jericho. And as He was leaving Jericho with His disciples and a large crowd, a blind beggar, Bartimaeus, the son of

Timaeus, was sitting beside the road [as was his custom]. When Bartimaeus heard that it was Jesus of Nazareth, he began to shout and say, 'Jesus, [a] Son of David (Messiah), have mercy on me!' Many sternly rebuked him, telling him to keep still and be quiet; but he kept on shouting out all the more, 'Son of David (Messiah), have mercy on me!' Jesus stopped and said, 'Call him.' So they called the blind man, telling him, 'Take courage, get up! He is calling for you.' Throwing his cloak aside, he jumped up and came to Jesus. And Jesus said, 'What do you want Me to do for you?' The blind man said to Him, 'Rabbani (my Master), let me regain my sight.' Jesus said to him, 'Go; your faith [and confident trust in My power] has made you well.' Immediately he regained his sight and began following Jesus on the road."

- Mark 10:46 52, AMP

When I think of our old friend, Bart, I'm instantly drawn to the overlooked reality that he was lonely. His story is one of miraculous faith, but if you notice, he was completely alone in the work of his fight. Let's dissect this passage, shall we?

First, we can see how easy it would have been for him to become a victim to his circumstance. Instead, we watch as he makes an intentional decision to do something about it. With judgmental labels that potentially followed him throughout his entire life, Bart had to eventually decide what came next. You see, in those days they believed your physical disability was the punishment of sin in your personal or generational life. So, from the beginning of his fight, people already believed that he was a loser.

Friend, it's one thing to believe something bad about yourself, but it's another thing when everyone around you agrees with it! If you read my book *#Unfiltered*, you know that I have a chapter titled, "Build". In it, I allude to the broken pieces of our lives becoming like badges that we wear throughout our journeys. They come to victimize us to become stuck in moments of our life in which we were never assigned to make a bed.

Maybe you're *resting in* some very real labels right now. Quite possibly, you've carried them for most of your life. Listen to me: the way you will lead yourself is in how you'll learn to grab ahold of promise or pain. You must have a BART moment by saying, "I'm sick and tired of being sick and tired!" You can't make a home out of a valley that God said you were only meant to move through.

* * *

Write it.

Yup, you know the drill. Grab that journal, friend, and let's do a quick challenge. I want you to set your alarm for two minutes and do a brain dump with me. Take some time to write down every label that others have placed on you. It can be factual or false, it truly doesn't matter. The bottom line is this: get every single label you can think of out of your head and onto that paper. It's important to understand what you've been believing so that you can recognize why you're getting the results you're getting. Are you ready? Set, anndd go, I'll wait.

Okay, now I want you to ask yourself this: "How am I agreeing with these things?" Circle the labels that you truly BELIEVE about yourself. Maybe there are things that you're not quite sure about, but still highly question. Go ahead and circle those too. Unless you emphatically disagree with them, they are an issue you need to address in the spirit.

Now, I want you to evaluate your page. Are you aware of how many things you believe concerning your situation? Are you shocked or pleasantly surprised with your belief system? Write some thoughts about this process and keep this page handy for the next steps that we'll take in our faith walk.

* * *

For an entire year before I was diagnosed with cancer, I was in and out of one doctor's office after another. I was only thirty years old at the time, but I felt more like seventy. In a constant state of grogginess, I found that I was sleeping fifteen hours a day and that I gained about twenty-five pounds in a matter of six months. No matter how little calories I ate, how many hours I worked out or how often I popped weight loss pills, the fact remained. Friend, I had high cholesterol, the scale wouldn't budge, and I was exhausted. For twelve months, I scheduled a monthly appointment, and every single time they would turn me away with no answers. After a year of blood work, diets, and testing, I succeeded in making myself look absolutely crazy.

"Mrs. Holt, you are healthy and vibrant! Nothing abnormal is showing in any of your results. I think we've concluded that you're simply depressed. Therefore, you have extreme fatigue and have managed to put on some weight." I remember going cross-eyed at this moment, "There's no way!" I blurted out, "I've married the love of my life only a year ago. I have moved to a place we love, we are traveling the world and my family is thriving. This is the happiest I've ever been!" It didn't take long before they answered me with a sharp, "Your body must be telling you that you're not as happy as you thought. There really is no other explanation at this point. I think you should consider taking this daily pill to help take the edge off. With all the sudden change in your lifestyle, your brain is having a hard time releasing the chemicals needed to function properly."

Friend, I remember leaving that office fully convinced that I must be clinically depressed. "Clearly, I'm crazy and nothing is truly wrong with me. My senses must have been off. I'm not truly happy, I'm depressed. I'm not truly sick, I'm perfectly healthy. They're right... life has been a whirlwind. I thought it was a crazy good kind, but I guess I need to just take the pill and stop with this mad rabbit chase concerning my health." Do you know what I did next? Yup, you guessed it. I took the pills. And you know what happened after that? The depression they said was manifesting, despite my picture-perfect life, turned into suicidal thoughts.

For two solid months, I took that little pill. And for nearly sixty whole days, my happy marriage became a space of torment while my life slowly morphed into some kind of reality that I despised. One afternoon after a huge fight with my husband, I ran into my room to do what most women do during these sorts of situations...cry it out.

I remember the posture I had at that moment. I probably looked a lot like lonely ole Bart sitting on the side of the road. I was labeled with false identity (depression) and my reality was beginning to agree with it. During my pity party, I can recall stumbling onto a worship LIVE while scrolling Facebook. I sat there sobbing, trying to explain to God how miserable my life was. The only problem was that I didn't understand any of it and my explanation became pure frustration, resulting in more of a meltdown.

It wasn't long until Bran walked into the room to check on me. A little offended that I chose to watch someone else's worship videos other than his, he made a joke about it hoping to make me laugh and gently said these words, "Love, I think you need to take some serious time to be with Jesus today. Don't leave this room until you've heard some answers concerning this emotional roller coaster you've been on. I have confidence in your ear to hear Him. I love you and I promise everything is going to be okay. I have the girls taken care of and I'll see you later this evening."

This was my personal Bart moment, friend. Faith met me in my fight, right there on my bedroom floor. It was the space where I realized I'd become sick and tired of being sick and tired. It didn't take hours or days to get my answer. In fact, all it took was one determined cry to Jesus. "Father, I need You to show me what is happening. Why am I feeling so hopeless and defeated? What is out of order in my body? I have searched for a year and everything seems to be getting worse! Open my eyes and help me see!" No sooner did the prayer exit my mouth did the answer hit my spirit. *Throw the pills down the toilet. This is not an emotional thing, it's a physical thing. Have faith and I'll reveal it to you.*

Immediately, I took my bottle of pills and flushed them down the drain. Afterwards, I ran down the stairs to Bran and told him what I felt the Lord said. We began to put our faith towards the hope that understanding was on its way. It hadn't even been a week until I had my first physical sign that led me to breast cancer. Not only that, but despite going off highly addictive pills (cold turkey) every suicidal thought had left my mind almost immediately.

Let me help you out here, winning the fight requires you to wake up! In verses 46-52, we can recognize four very specific steps that required Bart to wake himself into lasting faith. Very quickly we're going to break down this process together, and I hope that you'll take time to highlight this section so that you can revisit it when you need the reminder. Are you ready?

#1. When Bartimaeus heard, he spoke.

"When Bartimaeus heard that it was Jesus of Nazareth, he began to shout and say, 'Jesus, [a]Son of David (Messiah), have mercy on me!'"

- Mark 10:47, AMP

Friend, you might feel blind right now concerning the situation in your life. You could be saying, "Alissa, I don't see a way out of this at all." First, let me say this, faith begins where need is found. It's okay to recognize where you are, but are you willing to set your belief on where God is taking you?

Throughout this book, we've continuously reiterated the extreme need for using your WORDS! Did you know that the Bible talks about speaking 1,500 times? If you haven't picked up what I'm putting down, let me tell ya, it's a big deal!

To re-cap, we've discovered that faith cannot come unless we first hear, and hearing cannot happen unless we first speak (Romans 10:17). We also remember

Mark 11:23 saying that YOU must speak to YOUR mountain. In other words, speaking is necessary when it comes to winning a faith fight! I find it interesting that Bart couldn't physically see his answer, but he spoke out by addressing the answer himself. Remember this, declaration with expectation creates manifestation. Bart didn't have to know the how. He simply knew *WHO* was close by. "Jesus!" That's all it took to start leading himself differently.

Notice, he didn't call out to Jesus in a hopeful way. He called out to Him with expectancy! How are you speaking?

#2. Bart kept on.. all the more.

"Many sternly rebuked him, telling him to keep still and be quiet; but he kept on shouting out all the more, 'Son of David (Messiah), have mercy on me!'"

- Mark 10:48, AMP

I wonder how many of us keep on rather than giving up. Bart was surrounded by people who saw his trial as a losing battle. Rebuking his belief system wasn't enough for them, they also had to dictate what he was to do, "KEEP STILL! BE QUIET!"

I can only imagine the scene that took place. Jesus, on the move, 'ole Bart sitting on the street corner and a bunch of self-righteous followers who felt they knew what faith looked like. But it was a blind beggar who caught Jesus' attention. His fight had a winning spirit behind it. It refused to give up!

Friend, you must refuse to lose even when everyone around you is telling you to surrender. Faith ain't fair. It's a fight. When you feel the need to quit, keep on all the more!

#3. He threw his cloak aside.

"Jesus stopped and said, 'Call him.' So they called the blind man, telling him, 'Take courage, get up! He is calling for you.' Throwing his cloak aside, he jumped up and came to Jesus."

- Mark 10:49-50, AMP

During this time in history, a blind man's cloak was attached to his identity. It was often issued by the government marking them as legitimate beggars. Much like a driver's license gives permission to operate a vehicle, a cloak gives them the ability to collect alms. So often this was their only source of shelter and doubled as a mat for others to walk upon while scraping up any source of provision they could find.

Let's just call it what it is, a cloak was nothing more than a poor man's destiny. It shackled him to a future that no one ever wanted and gave people permission to believe that he was a loser. The significance in these verses was not the fact that Jesus stopped to call forth a beggar. It was that the beggar threw his only piece of identity off to the wayside. In other words, Bart was saying, "I'm not coming back here! You might see me as losing this fight, but I am winning. I have faith that I'm healed!" When you have lasting faith, you'll come to Jesus knowing that you're not returning the same way. Remember, the fight of faith threw the cloak aside before vision was ever given.

#4. "Let me regain my sight."

"And Jesus said, 'What do you want Me to do for you?' The blind man said to Him, 'Rabbani (my Master), let me regain my sight.' Jesus said to him, 'Go; your faith [and confident trust in My power] has made you well.' Immediately he regained his sight and began following Jesus on the road."

- Mark 10:51-52, AMP

What if I told you that faith is nothing more than permission for God to be God? When Jesus asked the question, Dart had an answer. He knew what he was believing and didn't hesitate to ask for it. When I was studying this scripture, the

Father told me to look up the definition for *let*.

let- *verb* /let/- to allow something to happen or someone to do something by not doing anything to stop an action or by giving your permission[4]

Immediately I was drawn to the part that placed responsibility on me: "... by not doing anything to stop an action or by giving permission." So many times, we treat our prayers as a game of Russian roulette. We load up on scripture and pull the trigger by making some declarations. All the while, we're standing there with our eyes closed wondering if the miracle is actually going to manifest.

Friend, you'll know you're in faith when you trust in God's power more than your pull. The fight is more about your surrender than it is your side throw. Give God permission to do what He does and get out of His way! You want to know how you receive the thing you're begging Him for? You let Him! You stop making excuses, you don't have a backup plan

[4] Cambridge Dictionary. July 2024. Cambridge University Press, 2024. https://dictionary.cambridge.org/dictionary/english/let?

and you make up your mind concerning your belief, deciding to throw your cloak and declare that your miracle is here!

* * *

Steps Towards Winning

Grab the page that we just dumped our cloaks (labels) onto earlier. Before we can continue this gnarly fight towards winning, we must address the losing battle. My husband always says, "The fruit will speak of the root. If you don't like what you see, you'll have to take an ax to the soil." This is where you dig in deep, my friend.

Believing that something is true authorizes it to produce in the spirit. This works for both faith and fear. Maybe you've heard the scripture before, "For God has not given us a spirit of fear, but power, love, and a sound mind" (2 Timothy 1:7, NKJV).

Did you know that fear is a spirit? Well, if God has not given us that spirit, then it must be demonic. So how can we identify the Spirit of God? Galatians 5 says the fruit of the Spirit is love, joy, peace, patience, kindness, goodness, faithfulness, gentleness and self-control. Simply put, if it's good, it's from God. If it's bad, it's from the enemy. How do I know this to be true? Everything the Father created in Genesis had a stamp of approval written in black and white: "It is good."

So much of our faith fight is wrapped up in self-evaluation. Ask yourself: What is hindering me and how do I position myself to receive? Once again, this is another opportunity for you to posture yourself correctly. If you fight *wrong*, you can't receive *right*. In order to win, you have to work the ring, and in most cases when it comes to faith, your mind is the battlefield.

Take some time and ask yourself what these "cloaks/labels" have been producing in your life. In other words, what fruit have you been seeing lately? Is it good or bad? Recognize the weaknesses and take an ax to the root system by praying over it.

* * *

Pray it.

Father, thank You for allowing me to let You do what You say You'll do in my life. The choice to nurture the fruit I produce is a huge responsibility, and I'm asking You to give me eyes to see and ears to hear concerning the miracle in my life. Today, I believe in You for lasting faith; the kind that does not wait to take hands with others, but leads the way on my own. I'm taking off the cloak of identity that has kept me sitting on the wayside. (Fill in the blank) _____ no longer dictates my future. I do not have to know how because I know WHO. I thank You for the strength to keep on when I want to give up. Help me to posture myself in a way that produces a fight that wins! In Jesus' name, Amen.

Chapter 7

Endurance

Journal

Hello,

It's the big day. I'm currently riding to the hospital with my husband praying as we enter this final step of our journey. In fancy words, I'm having a bilateral partial mastectomy with lymph node dissection. In simple words, I'm having a lumpectomy while taking several lymph nodes out for testing. Either way, this is a big deal. It's one of the biggest cages I'll step into as I swing the final punch for my title, which is a cancer-free report. Yesterday evening as I prepared for surgery day, I had a meltdown.

I arrived at Walmart for compression bras and antibacterial soap in a puddle of tears, and then a panic attack ensued. Funny enough, when I pulled into the parking spot, I recorded a nineteen-minute video to document my feelings. Later, I'd find that I hit the slow-motion button and my words were nothing more than a turtle stuck in peanut butter.

Something I said on the recording is worth noting, "Fighting with faith is a lot like juggling grief and gratefulness at the same time. I'm doing it while walking the tightrope called grace, and I'm trusting God in the process." Over the last twenty-four hours, I've found myself counting all my blessings and miracles that God has provided on this cancer journey.

1. I did not physically feel the second biopsy of my lymph node.

2. I had confirmation that the second tumor vanished with no explanation.

3. All 84 genes came back negative with a genetic test.

4. Six out of eight Zoladex shots were PAIN-FREE with 14-gauge needles.

5. Another suspicious spot miraculously vanished at a MRI biopsy.

6. My white and red blood count stayed at normal range through 16 rounds of chemo.

7. I never threw up once while on treatment.

8. I continued to travel, preach, worship and prophesy throughout treatment and Covid.

9. I began to grow hair back while still having six rounds of chemo left to complete!

10. The last tumor that remained in my breast miraculously dissolved even when they said chemo wasn't enough to shrink this type of cancer.

11. I didn't feel the antenna procedure in preparation for my surgery.

12. I never had more than two mouth sores the entire time I was on treatment.

13. Although I got Covid my last month of treatment, I didn't need to be hospitalized. The fluid on my lungs resolved quickly and my body did well, despite a compromised immune system.

14. God supernaturally provided financially, even with our entire careers shutting down due to Covid.

15. Our little family is closer than it's ever been. What was meant for evil has been used for good.

I saw a quote the other day that read, "You never know how strong you are until being strong is the only choice you have left." Today I feel the weight of that. Cancer doesn't give you a choice other than to fight. With two babies, a husband and a destiny that has yet to be fulfilled, I had no other choice but to fight! Through it, I've shared my journey with thousands of people around the world, prayed with hundreds of breast cancer patients and shared the hope of the gospel with doctors. Nothing goes to waste when you fight in faith and trust the Father with your future.

I sit in the waiting area now as I wait to be declared cancer-free. As unpleasant as surgery is, I have never been more ready for something in my life.

Today I come out victorious! I WILL WIN BECAUSE JESUS ALREADY WON!

-Alissa

Once the fog of anesthesia lifted, I was met by my husband's fingers running through the peach fuzz on my head. His voice sang over me with a song that became like our lullaby during this season:

Peace, peace, wonderful peace/ Coming down from the Father above/ Sweep over my spirit forever, I pray/ In fathomless billows of love.

Unable to open my eyes, I smiled at him as his words calmed my heart, "You did it, my love. The hardest part is over. Now, we go home to recover, and we can put this all behind us. Liss, you're my hero. You're the strongest person I've ever known in my life, sweetheart. I've wanted so badly to take this away from you, but you've shown me what faith looks like, and I'm proud to be your husband. Now, let's eat some good food and watch Netflix while you heal!"

The next thing I remember is waking up in my recliner surrounded by flowers and gifts. Bran and the girls did such a sweet job setting up our bedroom. Greeted with cards, smiles and encouragement, they stood over me with love and joy that this was over.

Home was a space of war for us. It was the place where I spent much of my time fighting for a future with my family, and over the process of eight months, my children and husband watched as I became painted pink in oncology offices and scarred with wounds none of us imagined I'd wear. Although it was gnarly, this specific day marked a win for us.

Later that evening, my husband helped me to the bathroom, and for the first time, I caught a glimpse of myself in the mirror. The cancer had covered me with fashion more than the flowered binder wrapped around my chest. With barely any hair, a swollen body, and blisters covering my stomach (due to menopause shots), I recognized the massive trauma my body had endured in a short amount of time. I wish I could say the scriptures taped to my mirror encouraged me at that moment.

The truth was I grieved from the depths of my soul when I truly took in the image looking back at me. I was bound up with pretty pink, but could still see the loss on one half of my chest underneath. Suddenly, I collapsed in my husband's arms and let out a gut-wrenching cry of pain. All the energy it had taken to fight this fight of faith flooded me with emotions. "It's ok, babe. Feel all of it. I'm here... I love you."

This is when my oldest daughter came into the room. I'll never forget it because her words pierced our hearts like knives. She isn't one to use many words in settings like this, but the spirit of faith rose in her ten-year-old heart. "Mom, you are doing this! You're beating cancer! You did something a lot of people wouldn't want to do. You saved your breasts. You made it through chemo. You are going through such a hard time, and I'm proud of you, Mom! You have shown so many people how to fight this and be brave with God. You can do this because you've already done so much. Don't be sad. They took the cancer out, and you're almost done. You know that I love you, right?"

In simpler terms, Kins was saying, "MOM, YOU HAVE ENDURED, SO CELEBRATE!"

Endurance- noun US /ɪnˈdʒʊə.rəns/

The ability to keep doing something difficult, unpleasant, or painful for a long time[5]

This definition brings to mind this scripture:

> "Consider it nothing but joy, my brothers and sisters, whenever you fall into various trials. Be assured that the testing of your faith [through experience] produces endurance [leading to spiritual maturity, and inner peace]. And let endurance have its perfect result and do a thorough work, so that you may be perfect and completely developed [in your faith], lacking in nothing. If any of you lacks wisdom [to guide him through a decision or circumstance], he is to ask of [our benevolent] God, who gives to everyone generously and without rebuke or blame, and it will be given to him. But he must ask [for wisdom] in faith, without doubting [God's willingness to help], for the one who doubts is like a billowing surge of the sea that is blown about and tossed by the wind. For such a

[5] Cambridge Dictionary. July 2024. Cambridge University Press, 2024.
https://dictionary.cambridge.org/dictionary/english/enduranc e?

person ought not to think or expect that he will receive anything [at all] from the Lord, being a double-minded man, unstable and restless in all his ways [in everything he thinks, feels, or decides]."

- James 1:2-8, AMP

Notice James did not say if you fall into various trials, he said *when* you do. In other words, it will happen, friend, so you should be prepared to consider it joy!

While studying this scripture, I heard the Holy Spirit urge me to take a deeper look behind the context of the word *fall*. It comes from the Greek *peripipto*, meaning "to fall into as to be encompassed."[6] One translation says "to be plunged or surrounded." So, we're not talking about tripping along the path of life. We're discussing the overwhelming action of what it means to find yourself in a position that looks to have no escape route. It's a distressful thing, and it

---

[6] Blue Letter Bible. July 2024. Blue Letter Bible, 2024. https://www.blueletterbible.org/lexicon/g4045/kjv/tr/0-1/

carries a sense of what it means to drown. You may be there right now and can feel the pressure on every side.

The question remains: how do you receive by faith in a crisis like this? Well, the scripture says that you must understand that the testing of your faith is for producing endurance for your fight! It says that endurance will have a perfect result that lacks nothing in your circumstance, and that He gives you wisdom to guide you through it.

The NKJV of the same verses say this: "My brethren, count it all joy when you fall into various trials, knowing that the testing of your faith produces patience. But let patience have its perfect work, that you may be perfect and complete, lacking nothing."

When we dive into the word *patience,* we see that it's derived from the ancient Greek root word *hupomone*. This signifies an active endurance and not a passive waiting stance. It's what it takes to actively finish a marathon, different from what it requires of you to patiently sit in the stand waiting for a winner. The ancient Greek Word *hupomone* comes from hupo (under) and meno (to stay, abide, remain). So, we can understand the context of the word *patience*, which means to remain under. It's the picture of someone remaining under extreme pressure and choosing to remain there despite the ability to escape.

Paul said in 2 Corinthians 4:8-9, NIV, "We are hard pressed on every side, but not crushed; perplexed, but not in despair; persecuted, but not abandoned; struck down, but not destroyed. Therefore, we do not lose heart. Though outwardly we are wasting away, yet inwardly we are being renewed day by day." The key here is to ask for wisdom in faith without doubting. James 1:8 says that doubters should not think or even expect to receive anything from the Lord because they're double-minded in their belief systems. In other words, God will give you everything you need to get through this with a WIN (lacking nothing), but your unbelief and inability to produce patient endurance will keep you stuck!

Friend, it's not your ability to carry the heavy load; it's your ability to remain when weakness comes. So often, we become enamored with big faith moves that we miss the steady pace of patient endurance. Let me ask you, what good is a giant step of faith if you have no longevity when it comes to stewarding the seed that you've planted?

I'm reminded of a Tiktok I recently saw of a man reflecting on a familiar passage in the Bible. Maybe you remember hearing about it in church; it's found in Matthew 14 and talks about a violent storm resulting in a man walking on water. The ending of this story became the beginning of spiritual aggravation for this social media influencer. He began to explain how bothered he was with Jesus' response to such a significant action of faith, "You of little faith, why do you doubt?"

"How could Jesus tell Peter how little faith he had when there was a boat full of other men unwilling to try it?" Suddenly, he heard the Holy Spirit tell him to google the definition of the word *little*, which he found.

lit·tle /ˈlid(ə)l/ adjective: A short time or distance.[7]

Little faith wasn't the measurement of how grand the faith move was. It was the time stamp on how long his patient endurance lasted.

There used to be a beach body coach I followed years ago. Her workout intervals lasted sixty seconds each, and her catchphrase was, "Anyone can do hard things for just one minute." I found this to be true in our faith fight. Anyone can hold on for short amounts of time, but a winner patiently endures even when the journey is long and drawn out. Friend, James says that the testing of your faith produces endurance. In other words, the hard thing is not what develops the faith needed to win. On the contrary, the hard thing reveals how much faith is actively available inside you to fight! I heard someone say it like this: if you feed your

---

[7] Oxford Languages Dictionary. Jan. 2024. Oxford University Press, 2024. https://www.google.com/search?q=definition+little

heart faith when you don't need it, your heart will feed your mouth faith when you do.

I have several friends who are marathon runners. I've never personally been one to find a lot of joy in these kinds of things, but trainers always amaze me with the discipline it takes for an event. With a minimum of twelve weeks of preparation, these athletes commit to building their lungs and legs for endurance. The goal is to get comfortable running three to four times a week, with their longest run being roughly five to six miles at a time.

Pushing oneself too fast could result in injuries, so finding a pace that works for the individual is essential. The same can be applied when it comes to faith. You can only expect to enter the race strong if you have trained for the strength needed and the timing to endure.

On the other hand, God isn't asking you to push yourself too hard or too fast either. Remember that mustard seed-size faith? James is not talking about the *bigness* of the faith fight; it's about the time it takes for that seed to produce some fruit!

Peter made a grand gesture by stepping out of the boat and walking on water, but his timing didn't outlast the storm! The waves created doubt, but ultimately, he didn't go the distance!

Timing is everything when it comes to life. It takes nine months to birth a baby, twelve years to get a diploma and eighteen years to be considered an adult. If we must *stick it out in* the natural, the same must be applied spiritually.

* * *

Write it.

Grab that journal, my friend! It's time to challenge our endurance. I have a saying that goes a little like this: you don't feel capable of anything significant because you've not been able to commit to anything small. Friend, significant wins make room for small victories. This is where I want you to celebrate your endurance thus far!

There's an old song we used to sing in kids' church, "Count your blessings, name them one by one/ Count your many blessings/ See what God has done." Throughout different seasons of my life, I can pull out journals and read my "blessing pages." This is where I quite literally count the things God has done for me (similar to the most recent journal entry I shared with you in this book). It doesn't matter how big or small; I write it down if it's a victory.

This is significant because we are built for progress. When we see the purpose behind what we believe in, it allows us to endure longer. My husband taught about this worldwide by equating it to worship. "Your worship will only carry you as far as your memory of God."

If you have experienced God the Healer, you will worship Him even when you're sick. If you've experienced God the Deliverer, you will worship Him even when you're bound. I want to carry this into your faith walk; your faith will outlast any fight if you recall the victories won with Jesus.

When I feel the load is too heavy, I pull the blessing pages out and remind myself of what God has already won in my life. Suddenly, I find a strength to endure much longer than I would have on my own. My family has sung a song through all the hell we've fought: "Your promise still stands/ Great is Your faithfulness/ I'm still in Your hands/ This is my confidence. You've never failed me..."

Friend, take time to number the battles you've won thus far. Every victory is worth celebrating, and every bit of progress is more punch for your fight! If He did it before, He will do it again!

Maybe you don't feel like there is much to record concerning the battles in your life. It could be that you don't truthfully see any victories in your history with Jesus. You may be getting started in this faith walk and haven't built enough stamina to list anything. I encourage you to start where you're at!

If you were in a position two weeks ago that had you questioning whether or not you'd make it to tomorrow, that is fourteen days of victories to celebrate! You are still here! If you've been depressed and unable to eat anything for days, celebrate a meal by recording a prayer, thanking God for a plate of food others might not have the blessing to partake in.

My point is this: there is always something to celebrate in life, even in the chaos of our wreckage. So take a second, number your page, and count the blessings God has gifted you with!

* * *

My great-grandparents were commercial fishermen and farmers throughout their marriage. As a young child, I remember spending the night with them in the country and waking to the smell of breakfast before the break of dawn. I didn't realize it then, but they were teaching me the importance of stewarding a seed with expectation and endurance.

With hundreds of acres of land, I recall watching my Papaw prepare the ground for planting. It was a long and challenging task, but the promise of production allowed the work to become a walk of faith. After planting the seeds, I remember Pa working the field until the harvest. From dawn till sundown, stewardship was required for a successful growing season.

I'll always remember my two favorite times of the year. The first was when I gathered all the supplies to help Grandma dress the scarecrow. We'd walk up and down the aisles of produce so Pa could track what had been snacking on their hard work. It amazed me how he could tell the difference between a bear, deer or coon. The second was when we gathered the harvest. All afternoon, our great grands would fill painter's buckets with food, and at the end of the day, we were rewarded with the pick of the field. With saltshakers and a hand towel in tow, we'd crack open watermelons in the garden and feasted like kings and queens.

I want you to see something here, friend; the reward could only have been enjoyed if the endurance was stewarded. It takes more than putting a tiny seed into the ground for fruit to come forth. Sleep had to be sacrificed, fields had to be worked and the seed had to be protected before the harvest could be collected. In other words, you can only be rewarded if you stewarded your soil correctly.

I've found that physical pictures often lead to spiritual truths. We want the promise of God's Word without exercising discipline. It just doesn't work that way, friend. If we must intentionally endure a physical growth process, we must be willing to endure a spiritual manifestation process.

The biggest lie to confront our faith is, *This is taking too long, so it must not be working.* If the enemy can encourage you to dig in the soil of faith before your seed grows roots, then he can cause you to abort the fruit from producing. In other words, the thought will come, but the timing is tested.

The will of God is always available in our lives, but our lack of faith can keep us from receiving the manifestation of it. At some point, we must stop blaming the devil for everything and realize that our faith is our responsibility to protect.

My grandparents didn't stand in the woods shaking their fists at the animals who partook of their crop. No, they knew that if they wanted it to stop, they had to take some steps to protect what was theirs. For us, that looked like gathering supplies, building scarecrows, dressing them up and believing our efforts would keep unwanted creatures out of our hard work. In faith, we do the same. We gather the Word, build our faith, dress our minds in new thinking and believe that God will do the rest!

I recently went on a trip to Arizona for ministry. After sharing my testimony and teaching for an hour on faith, you could tangibly feel the expectation for miracles in the room. After closing out my message, I heard the Holy Spirit say, *I'm going to heal bodies tonight. Obey Me, and I'll do the rest.* From there, the prophetic began to flow forth with words of knowledge concerning diseased and damaged areas in individuals' bodies. The altar was full of people who responded in faith. I began to lead them in a simple prayer toward receiving what God said was theirs. After they finished releasing a declaration of faith, I anointed my hands with oil and touched each individual, stating, "Be healed in Jesus' name."

Can I tell you something? We saw people healed of autoimmune diseases, tracheostomy complications, epilepsy and emotional trauma that night. Yet, the same room that housed the expectation for miracles is the same room that housed the opportunity for doubt.

While praying for individuals, I approached a lady who needed a creative miracle. I heard the Holy Spirit speak to me. *My will is to replace that which no longer works supernaturally, but ask her for what she wants to believe.* I took my hand off her head and whispered, "Can I ask you where your faith is? Do you want a creative miracle or doctors to help you?" She responded, "No, I want the doctors to handle it. I need a new kidney. I'm on the transplant list and am believing for surgery." Immediately, my spirit grieved knowing what the Father had spoken.

The opportunity for complete healing was available, but her faith is what agreed with the outcome. It's important to understand something when praying for others. The word is very clear that two or three must agree on Earth for it to come to completion (Matthew 18:19). We must recognize the responsibility we carry in prayer.

You cannot pray contrary to a person's will and expect your faith to overpower their belief system. Jesus said, "Your faith has made you whole" (Mark 5:34). In other words, you are the one who ultimately chooses what you receive. It is the honor of others to agree with you by linking their faith with yours.

At that moment, I had a choice: I could try to convince her to believe in a supernatural miracle, or I could meet her expectations. I am spiritually mature enough to recognize that the Father doesn't force us to receive anything we are not ready to accept. Instead, He leans into our small faith and proves Himself faithful with what we have available. Without condemnation, I chose to lay hands on her and spoke a prayer of completion over her surgical and physical needs. She began shouting and jumping all over that room because her faith believed this need was settled! My agreement became a seed planted towards her physical healing, and I believed I would get a phone call later stating, "The surgery went great!"

Another woman from this church could not be with us in person, but took time to watch the online service. Everything I have described to you, she saw first-hand from the screen of her phone. The next day, she testified of a spontaneous miracle she received from diabetes by simply doing everything I instructed those in person to do. By repeating the prayer, laying hands on herself and thanking Jesus for healing, she immediately felt a burning sensation on the right side of her body that was located under her rib cage. She thought it was strange but didn't think much about it the rest of the evening.

The following day, she took her blood sugar levels and was shocked to see the number 99 staring her in the face. She said this was the first time she had to adjust her insulin levels since she was diagnosed as a teenager. She felt led to google where her pancreas was in the body. Suddenly, she realized the burning sensation she had felt the night before was coming from the very place where her sugar levels developed. She worshiped and declared, "I've never felt anything like it! But I am healed!"

Once in Kentucky, I was speaking at a women's conference. At the end of my message, the Holy Spirit highlighted the spirit of infertility in the room. With direction from the Lord, I laid hands on a woman and began to speak a prophetic word that a child was on the way. I instructed her to speak over her womb by calling forth this baby's name and to get ready for completion.

I was told after service that this couple had been trying to have babies for years with no luck. I responded with, "Well, get ready. They will be soon!" Several months later, I received a Facebook message that included a picture of me praying over her and a picture of her announcing to her church that she was pregnant! It didn't look like God had answered at that moment, but He had begun a process in her body to prepare for the promise that was on its way.

Here we have a story of a woman who was met with hope despite her doubt, another who received an instant healing and someone who had to walk out a process before they saw the results. Regardless, faith was birthed in each one of them.

My point is this: there are many stages of growth in this five-letter word, but it all contains one major component:

you. You are the one who must believe. You are the one who must endure. You are the one who must receive what God has for you. The responsibility doesn't lie in a dramatic leap of faith; it develops over a span of time. In other words, when you refuse to give up, God refuses to let you down. He cannot contradict His Word, my friend. If He said it, I believe it, and that settles it. Endure until you see a result that speaks of His promise!

I don't know how to be anything other than authentic in this journey. One thing about a war is that there's no room for fake champions. At the end of the day, the proof is in the endurance displayed throughout the battle. The punches don't make the call. The knock-outs don't make the call. The body slams don't make the call. The one who endures makes the call, and that one can look bloody, sweaty and swollen at the end of the fight. There may be split lips, broken bones and black eyes, but when you get back up, when you swing the other fist, when you take another breath, when you regain consciousness, watch out! Because the final punch is what counts!

This faith process is about endurance, friend, not loss. Let me end this chapter by encouraging you with some scripture:

Favor finds you when you endure.
(1 Peter 2:19)

Perfect results, through work, spiritual maturity, inner peace, lacking nothing is produced through endurance.
(James 1:2-4)

A harvest comes for those who endure.
(Galatians 6:9)

Life is gained when you endure.
(Luke 21:19)

A way of escape and provision is found when you endure.
(1 Corinthians 10:13)

God's will and promise is found in endurance.
(Hebrews 10:36)

Blessed are those who endure
(James 5:11)

Friend, endurance means to suffer patiently. It's not a fun thing to do, but the reward is great! Consider these scriptures to be promises from God today. You have too much to offer this world to give up too early! You aren't losing; you're winning!

* * *

Steps Towards Winning

Friend, I hate to be the one to tell you, but this process never ends. You will win battles and overcome impossibilities, but your faith will continue to fight daily. When it comes to praying for an answer, it's easier to say God is denying us than it is to admit we have quit the race. I pray that this book gently debunks the lie of fear and increases the spirit of faith inside you. Still, I know that this is not always an easy process for us. So, for now, I will give you another practical step to win whatever battle you are up against.

Remember all those little blessings you counted earlier? What if all the answered prayers were to carry you through the uncertain moments? What if the memory of what God has done fuels the faith in what He can do?

I want you to take a second and actively sit in the thanksgiving of your heart. I'm not asking you to say a quick thank you; I'm challenging you to truly lean into your gratitude for everything collected on that page. There is something about stopping and sitting with Jesus. There is a posture that is taken when you intentionally take time out of the fight to feel the joy rather than the pain.

Today, I found myself in this position. With deadlines for projects, ministry dates booked up, homeschooling and navigating a unique journey in our life, I heard the Father say, "Stop and sit." I honestly didn't have time to sit, but I took a moment to escape to my back porch and breathe in the Florida breeze. With every breath I took, I found gratitude building up in my chest. I'm here. I'm alive. I'm grateful. Before I knew it, my spirit felt refreshed and my mind felt renewed. I went from overwhelmed and busy to overflowing and productive.

Today, stop and sit. Sit with your collected blessings and take time to feel the joy of all God has done. We will lose sight of the questions when we focus on the answers.

If He did it before, He will do it again. He did it for one, He will do it for me. If He promises me things, He cannot lie. Shift your focus today and breathe. I promise it will help you to endure the fight!

* * *

Pray it.

Father, thank You for allowing me to practice my endurance. However, it's not always easy. I know that timing is crucial for my growth in this storm. Help me prioritize the duration of my faith rather than simply considering the leap that is taken. Thank You for meeting my expectations and remaining faithful even when I can't physically see Your work behind the scenes. I rejoice in the answer before I receive it! Today, I make the shift, and choose to endure to see the end result of promise! In Jesus' name, Amen.

Chapter 8

Joy Unspeakable

Journal

8-18-22 (15 months later)

Hello,

Today is a day I've been dreading writing about. I've come to a decision with my husband and oncologist that I never thought I would make. The saving of my breast has been a huge journey, and now I'm at another crossroads. I feel as though I've failed in some ways, but then again, I see the warrior within me and understand that the battle scars tell the story of a winning fight. Even Jesus carried scars from the death of a process for us to speak of the victory of promise.

The past three months have been wrapped up in scans, phone calls, doctor visits and many prayer sessions. Despite the setback, I feel destiny written in this trauma. I cannot begin to pen the words my spirit has processed over the last ninety days, but I will try to convey the journey the best I can.

This past May was a time I will never forget. After a solid year of holistic treatment, healing my body and working through complex emotions with my very first therapist, I found the whisper of preparation calling out to me: *Alissa, you need a breast MRI.*

I thought this was strange. I had been doing intensive work with my integrative doctors, lost seventy pounds, went vegan, been in counseling and was more healthier mentally, spiritually and physically than ever. All my blood work seemed perfect, and my doctors didn't seem concerned. Still, the same voice I learned to recognize on my faith journey began to urge me to get a scan. When I mentioned the idea of this test to my team, they began to insist I get a mammogram instead. "Breast MRIs are not protocol. Insurance will not cover it, and we think it's unnecessary." Despite the consistent answers I received across the board from every professional I spoke to, I continued to hear the still-small voice, *You need a breast MRI.*

After much searching, I found someone willing to write me a script for out-of-pocket pay. My husband and I began to speak life over the results and put faith in our mouths by worshiping through the storm with praise. Only a short time had passed until I received the call that would change the trajectory of what came next. It hadn't even been a year since my lumpectomy, and I pictured this phone call looking much different than it went. I immediately took the call outside when I saw the doctor's name on my phone.

Bran was working at our business out of town, and the girls were inside doing homeschool assignments. I didn't know what to expect, but I wanted to be able to process it alone.

Without hesitation, he began, "Mrs. Holt, I just received your scan results. I'm highly suspicious that breast cancer is back, and I would like you to contact Dr. Williams as soon as possible to schedule surgery. I am sorry, Mrs. Holt, but a double mastectomy is in your best interest at this point." With a punch to the gut, I physically felt all the breath in my lungs escape. "A double mastectomy? You're sure of this without even having any biopsies performed?"

Tears immediately fell down my face as my heart raced into panic. Continuing to walk down the road, I heard the statement that solidified one of my biggest fears. "Like I said, I am highly suspicious. You have several areas that are showing up on your report, and my suggestion would be to do surgery immediately. Please make the phone call, or I can make it for you. This is very important. I would not advise that you ignore this."

Like a sack of potatoes, I dropped to the grass and wept. With the press of a button, we ended the call, and every bit of anger began to spill out of my mouth. "God, I'm so angry at you! How can You let me go through this again? I shared this journey with thousands of people around the world. They saw miracles, faith in action and gained hope. Why would You allow me to look like a fool now? I am done doing this Your way! Your way is not working. I'm exhausted." With a mascara-stained face, I began peeling myself off the grassy ground when I heard the Holy Spirit say, *Nice to know. We will do this your way now; let's see how that works.*

"God, You don't get it! You're asking me, as a woman, to sacrifice parts that make me feminine and to do it in HOPES that I will live longer." Immediately, I heard Him reply, *No, you don't understand. I sacrificed My Son in HOPES that you would believe in what He died for. Are you going to trust Me?*" Conviction gripped my heart in a moment of truth, and my words began to shift. "Father, You know this is the scariest thing You've ever asked me to do. I don't understand. Why is this happening? You said that I'd lose nothing; that was the promise. How are we here?" Suddenly, He began to speak to my heart in a way that transformed how I looked at this journey.

Alissa, I have never failed you. Every step of the way, I have proven who I am. If it weren't for the leading of My Spirit, you would never have received the grace to find these results the way you did. Please stop and list everything you have achieved through this journey. You have NOT lost! You've gained far more than you have ever sacrificed through this."

At that moment, I walked home, found my journal, sat on my back porch and made a list:

"Things I have gained through cancer, (MY WINS)

1. Peace

2. Wisdom

3. Freedom

4. Ministry to thousands

5. Forgiving myself

6. Confidence

7. Pride in who I am

8. Healing mentally and spiritually

9. Strength that I never knew existed

10. A WHOLE vibe rather than a broken mentality...

The list continued to fill the pages of my journal and tears of joy sprinkled the page. "Father, You are right. Cancer was the answer to so many questions in my life. What the enemy meant for evil, You used for good. Thank You for being faithful to me. I trust You. I don't understand, but I am leaving it in Your hands."

This decision wasn't easy, but I'm getting to know Peace, the person, a little more as I move forward with the process.

Bran and I have both cried over the past several days. We are making room to grieve together, but will still stand and fight again because celebration is on the way. Peace has been our compass throughout this entire journey. Even when it didn't make logical sense, the lean was not based on our own understanding.

He brought a knowing in our spirits concerning the path that we took. This is that. We feel the needle of direction and trust the One who guides our steps. He has never failed us; He won't start now.

-*Alissa*

It was sixteen days before my double mastectomy. My husband had surprised me with a family trip to a resort in Orlando. He knew that the recovery time would take months before I'd feel like myself again and wanted us to take intentional time to make some memories.

When we pulled up to registration, I was doing everything I could to fight off anxiety. This wasn't just a vacation for me. This would be the last time I'd join my family at a water park without feeling the absence of womanhood lurking over my shoulder.

The thought made me cringe, and the pit in my stomach grew heavy. Brandon had been such a support system throughout this entire journey. He loved me fiercely despite the bald head, chemo body and new scars. He'd always meet my insecurity with, "Liss, you're beautiful. I have eyes for no other. You have fought and won, and you're more breathtaking now than ever." Truly, I've been blessed to have a caregiver who loves me like Brandon Thomas Holt has.

Still, the uncertainty of this next step filled me with all the emotions as I sat and waited for him to get the keys to our room. While journaling some thoughts in the front seat, I heard a knock on my window. Brandon stood there with a woman I didn't recognize. He motioned at me with a massive smile. "Roll the window down; this lady wants to pray for you."

Confused, I opened the door and introduced myself. "Hi, I'm Alissa. How are you?"

"Hi, I am Nia. I met your husband at checkout. I mentioned that he looked like a singer, and he told me people call him

Vanilla Fred after Fred Hammond. He told me why you're here for vacation, and the Holy Spirit told me to pray for you. Would you allow me to lay hands on you and share what I hear in my spirit?"

The truth is, I was hesitant. So many people had laid hands on me, including myself. I had prayed, stood in faith, believed and shared the process with countless people. The questions stirring in my spirit were overwhelming, and the last thing I wanted was another "Keep on fighting" prayer to be prayed. Regardless, I gave her permission, and she pierced my heart with words I will never forget. I didn't know this woman, but my spirit bore witness to the fact that she knew Jesus. As she laid her hands on my chest, she began to pray prophetically for things of which she didn't realize the depths.

"I speak to cancer and everything that is out of alignment in Alissa's body. I call it back into alignment now in Jesus' name, for I hear you asking if this is another test. God says this isn't a test. It's not even a trial. This is, unfortunately, just life. Alissa, you're not being tested;

your faith is strong. God will use every bit of this and will not waste a thing. The thought of condemnation and the questions you have been asking are not of God.

"I hear the words: *recovery, recovery, recovery.* God will bring you through recovery, and I see you writing the steps in a journal. Every step of this journey has been written out. A book is coming out of this process, Alissa. In fact, you will write a book out of those journals, and it will strengthen people. It will help people heal and will allow them to recover in life.

"I speak to the lies that ask questions and speak prophetically that you will come through this with long life. God is using this for the sake of many. God is strengthening your body because you are coming out! Do not fear. Be of good cheer."

Tears rolled down my face as Bran stood in awe with a smile smeared across his face. I looked at her and said, "You have no idea what you're saying. We just discussed these questions on the ride to Orlando, and the journals you're talking about are in my suitcase. I was going to start my book this weekend while we were on vacation. I published another book out of journal entries, and the Lord told me this would be similar."

She smiled and wrapped me in a hug that brought healing to my troubled heart. This experience reminded me of where my "be of good cheer" has been located.

Friend, what if I told you that manifestation can't be met until joy is found? I know it sounds crazy, but the truth is that laughing in the face of fear can be the greatest display of faith. In other words, when you find joy, Jesus will meet you there. Don't believe me? Let's look at a scripture:

"Though now you do not see Him, yet believing, you rejoice with joy inexpressible and full of glory, receiving the end of your faith—the salvation of your souls."

- 1 Peter 1:8-9, NKJV

I know that laughing at a thing that brings sorrow, despair and pain can feel impossibly cruel. How can you possibly smile in the face of tragedy? Logically, it seems absurd! Still, scripture is clear that inexpressible joy is located smack dab in the middle of believing and receiving. Yet believing, with joy inexpressible, receives the end of your faith. In other words, you don't have an ending to what you're walking out of unless the sound of faith becomes joy in your mouth.

And let me clue you in: joy is not circumstantial; happiness is. Joy is found in none other than Jesus! It may seem impossible to be happy amid unforeseen tragedies, but it is possible to carry the joy of the Lord despite what you are living through.

Listen, if the enemy can keep you in your feelings, he can keep you out of faith. I did a whole chapter in my book #Unfiltered called "feels" and spoke on the reality of how feelings aren't fact, they're fickle. When walking by faith, we cannot allow our circumstances to determine our fighting stance.

Faith is steady and sound, my friend. You can stand on it, while emotions are things you get stuck in. Please hear me; we need to feel the things so God can heal them, but we don't have to stay there.

Our goal is not to rehearse the trauma in our lives; it's to rejoice in the truth that God will not fail us! If we believe, with joy, then we will receive our ending. God was precise in the equation for completion. He didn't make a mistake by placing joy in the middle. So we must understand the necessary ingredients for a finished work to come with a joyful sound that I win!

While studying the different versions of this scripture, I found it interesting that the New King James version says, "unspeakable joy." Unspeakable is defined as not being able to express in words. Another way to put it is there may not be an explanation, but there is a sound to follow!

My daughter and I snuggled in bed last night, scrolling Instagram reels. When she's having a rough night, she'll come to my room and say, "Mommy, can we watch funny videos before bed so we can laugh." It's always a good time to end our night with laughter in the air, and if you know us, you know that we laugh loudly.

Last night, there was a video that had us in absolute tears. We were laughing so hard that no words could escape our mouths. Rolling in bed, grasping for vocabulary, all we could do was hysterically laugh. There was no other sound for what we had just witnessed on that phone screen.

Kinsleigh came to the bedroom with a look of confusion on her face, and I held the phone in the air for her to watch the replay. Before we knew it, she had thrown herself on the bed and laughed uncontrollably with us. Friend, inexpressible joy doesn't need an intricate explanation, but the key is letting it out! You can't say you have joy while remaining quiet in your faith. There is a sound that must come forth.

Let me ask you this: if Jesus said it is finished, then don't you already have it? It's time to celebrate on layaway, my friend! You may have to make spiritual payments while placing your faith on credit. It may take a minute to lay your hand on the thing you're waiting for, but at the end of the day, it's yours, so rejoice!

Throughout many seasons of my life, I've had to learn how to laugh on layaway, knowing that the end result was on its way. Sure, it might have made me look a little crazy, but the equation for receiving doesn't place joy at the end. It's written in the middle for a reason, and the more I study scripture, I find joy laced within significant breakthrough moments, and it's documented for our encouragement. Let's take a look at several examples in the Bible.

Paul and Silas had a journey of joy in Acts 16. If you've read this passage, you know it begins with Paul having a vision in the night hour. He shares how he saw a man pleading for help in Macedonia. The following day, Timothy and Luke joined him on a mission to preach the gospel in that area.

Many miracles took place along the way, but one changed the trajectory of their journey. A demon-possessed woman began to scream out, "These men are servants of the Most High God! They are proclaiming to you the way of salvation!" (v17). She continued to scream at these men for several days until Paul became incredibly annoyed with her. Without hesitation, he turned to her and spoke, "I command you in the name of Jesus Christ to come out of her!" At that very moment, the woman was set free.

You'd think this moment of deliverance would be a sign to those watching the situation that God is real and that salvation is necessary. Instead, the owners of this woman became extremely angry. They were using her vexed spirit to make money off of her fortune-telling. Once they saw she had been released from the demons, they knew their income had been cut off.

Immediately, they seized Paul and Silas, dragging them before the authorities, demanding they be punished for disturbing the peace of the community. The crowd began to join in the attack and the chief magistrates tore Paul and Silas' robes, ordering them to be beaten with rods. Once they had been severely wounded, they were thrown inside an inner dungeon and fastened with chains around their ankles and wrists in agonizing positions.

Let me ask you, do you think these men had a right to turn their backs on God? After all, God was the one who gave Paul a vision, leading them in a direction that caused destruction in their life. How many times have we felt the leading of the Father only to have an unfortunate event meet us with pain and agony?

I'm curious what your knee-jerk reaction would have been if it were you in those moments. Would your response to God be laced with doubt and fear? I think it's safe to say that these men had every right to feel abandoned, abused and angry. Still, their response is one we can note on our walks of faith.

Paul and Silas did not shake their fists at God in this situation. Instead, they met joy in the middle of faith with a sound that shook the prison. Scripture says at about midnight, Paul and Silas were found praying and singing hymns of praise to God. Despite their circumstance, they chose to find a sound of joy to fill the atmosphere of that dungeon room. The Message version of Acts 16:25 says that they sang a robust hymn to God. In other words, this song was not a weak cry of defeat. It was a strong and healthy sound of joy!

Suddenly, without warning, a massive earthquake shook the prison. Every door flew open, and every chain holding each prisoner was loose. Startled from sleep, the prison guard saw all the doors open wide and assumed they had all escaped. Pulling his sword, he prepared to kill himself when he heard Paul's voice, "Don't do that! We're all still here. No one has run away." The guard was so shaken he ran inside, collapsing at Paul's and Silas' feet.

With a prayer of salvation, they saw the guard come into kingdom knowledge as he spent the rest of the night serving the prisoners by dressing their wounds, preparing a feast and introducing his family to them. The entire prison was in celebration despite the circumstances! All because a sound was heard in the middle of believing and receiving.

David is another example of what it looks like to showcase unspeakable joy in the face of sacrifice. In 2 Samuel 6, we read about a bloody process covered in unbelievable praise. Its purpose was to transport the Ark of the Covenant into Jerusalem. The ark represented the manifested presence of God and sacrifice was essential for transportation. To accomplish this task, David gathered thirty thousand men from Israel. They placed the Ark of the Covenant on a cart and brought it from Abinadab's house, which happened to be on a hill. While moving the ark, they came to Nacon's threshing floor, and the oxen stumbled, almost overturning it. A man named Uzzah reached out to catch it, and the anger of God struck him dead.

David was furious at God for having an outburst due to irreverence and began to grieve. Once this took place, he began to question the command of the Lord, "How can the Ark of the Lord come to me?"

He was scared to move it after seeing death become a consequence. So he left the ark at the house of Obed-edom for three months.

The scripture talks about how blessed their household and family were due to the manifested presence dwelling on the ark. David heard about how this affected this family and decided to complete the job of delivering the ark into the city of David. Only this time, he placed a demand on sacrifice and joy while navigating the middle of his journey.

While rejoicing with gladness, David danced vigorously with loud tambourines, cymbals, harps and lyres. While releasing a sound that spoke of unspeakable joy, those who carried the Ark of the Lord walked six steps and slaughtered an ox and fatling. If you can picture this correctly, you'd see an entire voyage that ran with the streams of blood from the sacrifices. It was marked with the dead carcass of many animals and smelled of death. Still, the sound of joy rang through the atmosphere, and David ushered the presence of God into the City of David with a sacrifice of praise.

Upon arrival, the scripture says his wife, Michal, looked down from the window above and saw her husband leaping and dancing in his priestly garments (2 Samuel 6:16). The sound must have caught her attention, but the disdain and contempt she felt in her heart kept her mouth from praising alongside him.

David entered the city by throwing a party with an entire multitude of Israel. The Lord had been faithful, and the ark had safely arrived at his kingdom. When he returned home, his wife met him with a sarcastic statement, "How glorious and distinguished was the king of Israel today, who uncovered himself and stripped off his kingly robes in the eyes of his servants' maids like one of the riffraff who shamelessly uncovers himself!"

David's response spoke volumes, "It was before the Lord that I did this, who chose me above your Father and all his house, to appoint me as ruler over Israel, the people of the Lord. Therefore, I will celebrate in pure enjoyment before the Lord. Yet, I will demean myself even more than this and will be humbled in my own sight and yours, as I please, but by the maids whom you mentioned, by them I shall be held in honor" (2 Samuel 6:21-22). The scripture says that Michal was prophesied to conceive no children until her dying day due to judging the joy displayed on David's journey of faith.

Friend, hear me good; people will get offended when your faith moves begin to make joyful sounds. Radical praise will cause broken people to retaliate. I'll never forget the many moments when others would rather watch me fail than watch me heal. Specifically, while sharing the middle of my cancer journey, many people would roll their eyes, send me mail stating that I was cursed and leave hateful comments on social media. The bottom line remained a solid ground for me to stand on, *I win* remained my mantra and praise continued to be my fighting stance.

The unspeakable joy displayed in the middle of my circumstance allowed the faithful end to be proven. Much like David, the journey required blood, cutting and sacrifice. The woman I always knew myself to be died on that operating table, but the shout in my mouth remained steady. I win because Jesus won!

Do you know what laughter does to you medically? Science has proven the enhancement of lung, heart and muscle health when you laugh. In turn, endorphins released to your brain activate and neutralize stress responses. They've also found that laughter improves circulation, can reduce pain levels and reduces artery inflammation. In other words, laughter not only heals your soul but can heal your physical body. Now we can understand the scripture, "The joy of the Lord is your strength," a little more clearly (Nehemiah 8:10). Friend, the enemy is after your joy because he knows once joy comes, manifestation follows!

Laughter is contagious for a reason. It is a lifeline to the final step in our faith walk. If God can get joy through you, He can get answers *to* you! Yet believing, with joy inexpressible, allows us to receive the end result of our faith.

During this season with cancer, my parents sent me many teachings by Mark Hankins. One collection of messages included laughing classes. Yes, you read that right. He broke down the necessary element of healing found in our joy and shared how cancer patients at MD Anderson are taught how to laugh as part of their treatment plan.

On my bad days, Brandon would find me sitting alone and crying. Out of nowhere, I'd crazily state, "Ha! Ha! Ha!" At first, he looked at me confused, "Babe, what in the world are you doing?" I responded, "HA! HA! HA! I'm done questioning God; I'm laughing instead! HA! HA! HA!" It didn't take long for the contagious laughter to roll out of our mouths. Suddenly, we found ourselves belly-laughing at the ridiculousness of the situation. It may have started out as forced, but it ended with an atmosphere full of joy!

Laughter is the medication for your miracle. Sometimes, you must laugh on layaway, knowing that your answer is on the way! If you win, then stop sitting around like a loser. You must find your victory cry!

* * *

Write it.

Friend, grab that journal! It may not seem like much, but I want you to brain-dump all the silly things that bring you joy. Is it a comedy show? Maybe you're like my daughters and love funny cat videos. It could be a simple cup of coffee while watching the sunrise. Or perhaps you love to sing in the rain.

Take a moment and pen the simple things that make you smile. Perhaps it's breakfast with your family or walks around the park. Maybe it's playtime with your children or cooking dinner with your favorite person. It doesn't have to be profound; it just has to be a list of the things that open your eyes to find joy in the journey. You may feel like you're in the middle of hardship, but you'll remain stuck until you take a second to find unspeakable joy.

While preparing for my double mastectomy, the Holy Spirit reminded me of a story in the book of Acts 27. I've heard many sermons preached on this scripture, but the light bulb didn't click until that day. It starts with a group of prisoners setting sail to Rome. Among those in captivity was Paul. He had been arrested for preaching about Jesus' saving grace. Over many days, they boarded three different ships while navigating rough waters. While on land in Fair Havens, Paul warned them prophetically of what was to come, "Men, I can see that our voyage is going to be disastrous and bring great loss to ship and cargo, and to our own lives also." Still, they ignored his urgency and listened to Pilate and the owner instead. Boarding a fourth ship, they loaded all the prisoners and passengers and set sail again.

This is where things got sticky, my friends, let's read:

"When a gentle south wind began to blow, they saw their opportunity, so they weighed anchor and sailed along the shore of Crete. Before very long, a wind of hurricane force, called the Northeaster, swept down from the island. The ship was caught by the storm and could not head into the wind, so we gave way to it and were driven along. As we passed to the lee of a small island called Cauda, we were hardly able to make the lifeboat secure, so the men hoisted it aboard. Then, they passed ropes under the ship itself to hold it together. Because they were afraid they would run aground on the sandbars of Syrtis, they lowered the sea anchor and let the ship be driven along. We took such a violent battering from the storm that the next day they began to throw the cargo overboard. On the third day, they threw the ship's tackle overboard with their own hands. When neither sun nor stars appeared for many days, and the storm continued raging, we finally gave up all hope of being saved.

"After they had gone a long time without food, Paul stood up before them and said: 'Men, you should have taken my advice not to sail from Crete; then you would have spared yourselves this damage and loss. But now I urge you to keep up your courage, because not one of you will be lost; only the ship will be destroyed. Last night, an angel of the God to whom I belong and whom I serve stood beside me and said, 'Do not be afraid, Paul. You must stand trial before Caesar; and God has graciously given you the lives of all who sail with you.' So keep up your courage, men, for I have faith in God that it will happen just as he told me. Nevertheless, we must run aground on some island.'"

- Acts 27:13-26, NIV

Notice, the angel never told them they wouldn't shipwreck. He promised they would not die. I wonder how many of us have said something to the extent of, "If it's God, then it will be supernaturally handled." We believe that the handprint of deity is found within the undeniable miracle of a thing. The problem is that our idea of miracles is different from God's idea.

So many times, I've witnessed lives that have seemingly *shipwrecked*. Far too often, hearts become hardened, and bitterness takes root in the idea that God didn't answer prayers. When dissecting Paul's voyage, we can learn a lot about how we navigate ours.

First, walking with the Lord gives way for the warning of the Lord. Paul saw what was coming because the Holy Spirit gave him wisdom. So many times, we are caught off guard because we are not taking the time to hear. Every time I've had a significant shipwreck, I can recall the spaces where the Holy Spirit lovingly prepared me ahead of time. Not always did I understand what was taking place, but in every single place, I could look back, in hindsight, and see the hand of the Father at work in my life.

Friend, it's not His intention to keep you in the dark. Open your eyes by faith and allow Him to position you for the journey.

Second, faith doesn't guarantee storms won't come. It didn't matter how prepared Paul was for the shipwreck awaiting him. The hard truth is that it was part of his assignment. Yes, Paul was warned, but don't you think God saw the disobedience before they had a chance to respond? Still, He was good enough to give them a heads-up, knowing they wouldn't listen. You'd think He would show grace towards Paul and supernaturally disintegrate the hurricane, but He didn't. Instead, He sent an angel to build faith in an impossible situation. "The storm will cause a shipwreck, but you won't die!"

Third, we see a command during the chaos, "Be of good cheer!" In other words, make a sound that contradicts the chaos you are facing. Paul said, "I see what's on the other side of this storm, so we must celebrate! Don't cry. Be cheerful! God is on our side!" Sometimes, faith looks like drowning while continuing to dance.

As a Florida resident, I know how serious it can be when hurricanes are advertised. The fact that this storm had been given a name showed how powerful it was. Still, joy was required for the journey. How many of us have been calling the name of our storm rather than confiding in the name of Jesus? Be of good cheer! He promises that you win!

Fourth, the receiving of a need is always stewarded in the middle of the thing. Paul was found in the middle of a sea. He was surrounded in the middle of a storm. In the middle, the angel found him with the command to find unspeakable joy! The decision was placed in the hands of those sitting on the ship. Would they focus on the storm or the Savior? Today, the decision remains yours. Will you steward the middle of this journey the way God says or your storm says? Choose joy!

The remainder of Acts 27 shares a story of a shipwreck, a promise and a new beginning. After sitting in an isolated storm for fourteen days, the men sensed land approaching. Rather than escaping, Paul gave thanks, broke bread and encouraged them to gain strength by eating together. When daylight came, the ship struck a sandbar, tearing it into pieces and leaving the men stranded at sea. Holding onto planks and stray pieces of the boat, they were able to reach land.

The shipwreck was inevitable, but the promise was undeniable! Not one person lost their life, just as the angel had said. From there, we see a beautiful story of a healing revival that took place. Every person on the island was healed of disease and confessed the power of God, but they wouldn't have known of God's healing power if it weren't for the shipwreck!

Friend, when my double mastectomy came my way, I sat in the grass, begging God to take the storm away, and guess what? He didn't promise me a supernatural way out; He reminded me of the prophetic word I received initially: *This will not be unto death. It will be for my glory.* I wonder how many of you have been holding onto broken pieces of your life while begging God to take them away. Can I tell you a secret? He assigned you to this storm, and once you catch the spirit of faith, you can laugh in the face of fear, knowing that you win on the other side of this! God doesn't promise you that pieces won't fall, but He promises to put them into place. The loss of the ship could not compare to the gain of the island. Revival came at the expense of an uncomfortable situation.

The morning of my surgery was full of contagious laughter. Bran and I woke up at 6am and began our hour-long commute to the hospital. With the sun rising around us and worship filling the car, we joked with each other more than we had in years. An atmosphere of peace brought cheer in a chaotic moment for us. We weren't sure what to expect, but we knew that the shipwreck was scheduled just hours from now. Still, we took joy in the promise that I would live and not die.

With one hand on the steering wheel and the other reaching for my hand, Bran looked me in the eyes with the sound of rest in his voice. "Babe, the end of night is the start of morning. We are stepping into a new day! Be at peace, my love." From there, we found out just how powerful the middle of our journey could be. Faith has never been fair, but the fight became laughter on our tongues. We were assigned to this storm, and a movement has been birthed out of a mountain we never foresaw climbing.

With thousands of lives watching us navigate this season, we've had the opportunity to partner with diseased, hopeless and emotionally broken people. We'd released a word of hope and love over their lives and had shown them how to take a hold of faith with a winning attitude that refuses to lose. Friend, it's the same for you.

You're assigned; you've not been abandoned. I know you'd rather see a supernatural miracle, but maybe God is calling you to a sacrificial movement. Perhaps this is so much deeper than you. Maybe your story is called to save the lives of many while proving just how good God is. Here's the truth: this faith fight has never been about you; it's always been about HIM. He won so that you could win, and you win so that you can share the gospel of a living God with those around you. Be of good cheer.

* * *

Steps Towards Winning

Friend, we have cultivated a journal habit, created vision boards, prepared healing scriptures and counted our blessings. This one is probably my favorite of all the steps I've shared with you. From the moment cancer started, God began to challenge my ability to celebrate. Throughout the process, He continually reminded me to be of good cheer and allowed me to reflect on the goodness of all He's done. Remember, you can't win unless you intentionally decide not to lose! This project was my way of recording every single winning moment along the way, and I hope you will do the same.

When Bran and I married, he gave me a beautiful leather journal. It was wrapped in a strap and came with beautiful antique-looking pages. Paired with a handwritten letter, his groomsmen delivered it to my dressing room. Some of the words he penned read, "I wanted to commemorate this auspicious occasion by giving you your first new journal for this journey. I pray that these pages will be full of joy, peace, pains, love, angry moments, lessons learned and most of all... VICTORIES! Fill these pages with the story of *US*. I'm recklessly in love with you."

I never wrote a word in this leather-bound book until I was diagnosed with breast cancer. The Holy Spirit spoke to me and said: *This is your joy in the journey journal. Post pictures, write funny stories and document the LIFE that is present despite the death that has tried to raise its head.*

With Polaroid pictures and snapshots from my phone, every page is documented with moments that bring smiles to our faces. Every victory shared and little moments caught lives within the pages of my wedding gift. I have stuffed that journal full of memories for three solid years until it's overflowing with evidence that God is real. I never imagined how *thick* our victories would be until I began to piece together the pages with Jesus.

My family will cherish this journal for the rest of our lives. Photos, stories and inside jokes line the paper with priceless proof that God never fails, even when we feel He has. If ever we need a reminder of how faithful He has been, it's as close as the flip of the page.

My challenge to you is to do the same. Create moments and memories by documenting the joy along the way. It doesn't have to be grand or fancy. We have family cuddle snapshots, and photographed moments on the lake, and breakfast at the table. Every space tells the story of LIFE despite the thing that is trying to choke out purpose... that is what we recorded. Start today; I promise you'll look back and smile, knowing one thing: you win.

* * *

Pray it.

Father, I thank You for the opportunity to laugh in the face of fear. I speak celebration over the storm in my life and replace the name of (fill in the blank) _____ with victory. Thank You for continuing to strengthen the weak areas in my life. Please help me to see the assignment You have placed me on rather than the destruction I am navigating. Thank You for trusting me with this journey. Use every bit of this season and allow it to bring revival to the hearts and lives of those around me. I'm asking that You help me remember those things from which You've saved me. I pray You get the glory every time I recall the faithfulness of Your hand in my life. In Jesus' name, Amen.

Chapter 9

Bonus Letter

Journal

11-19-22

Hello,

It's an odd thing when grief and celebration collide. I have felt the peace of Jesus right here simultaneously in the midst of loss and victory. It's pretty interesting because I never thought I could ever feel the weight of grief paired with the joy in celebration at the same time.

I got my pathology reports back yesterday. I am cancer-free. I specifically prayed and prophesied over myself while recording voice memos I could listen back to, "Every lymph node will be clear. My chest wall will be clear of cancer. Every spot will come back benign or stage zero DCIS with no invasive cancer found. I will require no chemo or radiation for further treatment. I am cutting the head off the giant once and for all with a victory that I WIN." Today, I can record a definite answer to prayer as every one of those things was confirmed with testing from my surgery.

I did not doubt that Jesus was faithful, that He'd been good and that He kept His promises. Still, the paper proof aligning with the report of the Lord brought me so much victory. Yesterday, I sat in my recliner and turned on CeCe Winans' song, *Believe*. I let tears of peace flow while speaking, "You said it, I believe. It is done." I'm overwhelmed with gratitude.

Next week, we gather with the family for Thanksgiving, and I feel so much praise wrapped in peace, knowing we've cut the head of the giant off once and for all. Repayment is on its way; an accelerated restoration for everything that has been lost in this journey; even for our five years of marriage. What the enemy has tried to steal from Bran and me the moment we got together... the repayment, the gain. I feel an expectation in my spirit that I haven't felt in a long time.

I've not fully felt rest that this battle was over since the moment I began. I had peace that it would not kill me, but I hadn't experienced the "it's done" until the final surgery took place. I have an overwhelming knowing in my soul that this will never touch me again. The spiritual battle has been fought; the physical battle has been won. I haven't seen myself physically yet. I'm bandaged up and wrapped tightly. The mental battle attached to double amputation is very real. I'm not ready to see myself quite yet. Still, I know the Lord will help me overcome that in Jesus' name.

Jordana Filkey prophesied over me the night before my surgery. "Alissa, the Lord will reconstruct your mindset in how you see yourself despite the choice not to be reconstructed with surgery." Even when I see myself for the first time, I believe there would be such love for my new body. Instead of disdain, grief or mourning, life and femininity would be celebrated. Even when the world tries to tell me that I lost a part of my body that speaks of womanhood, that out of the loss, a lioness would reign. Out of the battle, I would feel a sense of belonging I have never felt before. Indeed, I have won because Jesus wins; certainly, His goodness and mercy have followed me all the days of my life. He has kept His promises (Hebrews 10:23).

Jesus had been so good. I claimed Nahum 1:9: This current affliction would not occur twice. I had spoken this over myself daily for the past two years. At first, I thought, *God, how am I back in this position when Your Word says different?* Now, I see that He is a promise keeper. The current affliction didn't occur twice.

Compared to the first time, this last time was a much different circumstance. No long-term chemotherapy or radiation was needed. Invasive cancer was not present in my body this time around, and the journey was over with one surgery. It may not have been what I ever imagined for my life, but He kept His word.

Today, I am speaking a prayer over my life: *This is done in Jesus' name. It will never touch my body again. It will not shift, move, migrate or breathe ever again. I will not live bound to fear and the memory of disease. I will fully celebrate life as I take others by the hand and declare we win! Thank you, Jesus!*

-Alissa

Bonus Letter

Dear Friend,

While writing this book, my prayer was not for the masses nor the influence, but for you. If I could take you by the hand and listen to the stories surrounding your faith, I would. Your fight is necessary for more than surviving. It carries the message of hope for others to win despite the giant standing in their way. I wish I could promise you a life free of pain. The truth is pain teaches us about our purpose. Even Jesus begged the Father for an escape route when completing the assignment on His life. "Nevertheless, it is not my will; Your will be done" (Luke 22:42). God's will came laced with death, but spoke of new life. The winning stance may not look miraculous initially, but it always ends with victory.

If you follow my story online, you know my faith journey is incomplete. Nearly four and a half months after my mastectomy, my loving husband moved in with Jesus and made Heaven his home. Almost two days before his passing, I stood beside his hospital bed with victory in my mouth. With my fingers combing his hair, I spoke these words over him, "We've done it before. We'll do it again." I lifted his arm and pointed to the matching tattoos on our forearms. *He won = I win.*

"Brandon Thomas, no one can tell us any different." With the squeeze of my hand, he smiled and went to sleep. It was one of the last conversations we'd have, yet the power behind it remains.

I wish I could explain why things happen the way they do. The bottom line is this: it's not my job to change my theology based on my personal life experience. Nor is it my responsibility to make it all make sense. The only question I'm accountable for is, "What do I believe?"

From the very beginning of our relationship with Christ, belief was required. It's the thing that unlocks miracles and the single most important ingredient needed for purpose. Our faith cannot be activated without an active belief system, and let me remind you, without faith, it's impossible to please God (Hebrews 11:6). God never promises us a faith that's fair. He very clearly states that faith comes in the form of fighting. You must continue believing the victory is yours despite the hardship thrown your way.

Friend, this present suffering cannot compare to the glory revealed through this! I know it can be unbelievably difficult, but only you can stand your ground. Don't you dare give up! You must find some righteous anger and take back everything the Word says is yours.

My last words of wisdom would be this: YOU are the answer to your breakthrough. Jesus can't touch what you don't allow Him to. Stop expecting God to fight for you when you don't even fight for yourself. This journey called faith never ends! When you think you've won a victory, another battle will knock on your door. This is not meant to discourage you but to encourage you to stay alert. Do not waver.

Your faith cannot be rooted in feelings, and your fight cannot be inconsistent. No matter what comes, the Word of the Lord must be the declaration of your mouth. God said it, I believe it, and that settles it! I'm not nearly done with my journey, and neither are you. In fact, we're just getting started.

The plans might have changed, but the promise remains the same. I hope you follow me on social media so I can keep up with your story! This is where the giant falls and your victory will be heard! I'm cheering you on from the sidelines and can't wait to celebrate with you! We win!

P.S. I'm officially two-years cancer-free! Bran may not be here physically, but the girls and I will take him with us in our hearts as we celebrate in Bora Bora just like we said we would.

With all my love for coffee,

-Alissa

Healing Scriptures

These are the Scriptures that I read every day and then made faith declarations, based on the confession. The Word must get down into your heart and then must be spoken through your mouth for the healing transaction to be completed!

So then faith cometh by hearing, and hearing by the word of God.

- Romans 10:17, KJV

But what saith it? The word is nigh thee, even in thy mouth, and in thy heart: that is, the word of faith, which we preach;

That if thou shalt confess with thy mouth the Lord Jesus, and shalt believe in thine heart that God hath raised him from the dead, thou shalt be saved. For with the heart man believeth unto righteousness; and with the mouth confession is made unto salvation.

- Romans 10:8-10, KJV

My son, attend to my words; incline thine ear unto my sayings. Let them not depart from thine eyes; keep them in the midst of thine heart. For they are life unto those that find them, and health to all their flesh.

- Proverbs 4:20-22, KJV

We must take the Word like medicine! At least three times a day! We must read scripture and then make our confession (release our faith) through our words! God's Word must become more real to us than the sickness or disease that is manifesting in our bodies.

God is our refuge and strength, a very present help in trouble.

- Psalms 46:1, KJV

Jesus the Healer is more present than the trouble- the symptoms of sickness or disease. We must get our eyes on Him (The Word).

In the beginning was the Word, and the Word was with God, and the Word was God.

John 1:1, KJV

And off of our symptoms. We must renew our minds!

And be not conformed to this world: but be ye transformed by the renewing of your mind, that ye may prove what is that good, and acceptable, and perfect, will of God.

\- Romans 12:2, KJV

Healing is ours! We must receive it by faith!

We having the same spirit of faith, according as it is written, I believed, and therefore have I spoken; we also believe, and therefore speak;

- 2 Corinthians 4:13, KJV

If ye abide in me, and my words abide in you, ye shall ask what ye will, and it shall be done unto you.

- John 15:7, KJV

Therefore I say unto you, What things soever ye desire, when ye pray, believe that ye receive them, and ye shall have them.

- Mark 11:24, KJV

For this reason I am telling you, whatever you ask for in prayer, believe (trust and be confident) that it is granted to you, and you will [get it].

- Mark 11:24, AMP

And this is the confidence that we have in him, that, if we ask any thing according to his will, (His Word) he heareth us: And if we know that he hear us, whatsoever we ask, we know that we have the petitions that we desired of him.

-   1 John 5:14-15, KJV

And said, "If thou wilt diligently hearken to the voice of the LORD thy God, and wilt do that which is right in his sight, and wilt give ear to his commandments, and keep all his statutes, I will put none of these diseases upon thee, which I have brought upon the Egyptians: for I am the LORD that healeth thee.'

-   Exodus 15:26, KJV

And ye shall serve the LORD your God, and he shall bless thy bread, and thy water; and I will take sickness away from the midst of thee. There shall nothing cast their young, nor be barren, in thy land: the number of thy days I will fulfill.

   - Exodus 23:25-26, KJV

I call heaven and earth to record this day against you, that I have set before you life and death, blessing and cursing: therefore choose life, that both thou and thy seed may live...

   - Deuteronomy 30:19, KJV

There failed not ought of any good thing which the LORD had spoken unto the house of Israel; all came to pass.

   - Joshua 21:45, KJV

Not a word failed of any good thing which the LORD had spoken to the house of Israel. All came to pass.

   - Joshua 21:45, NKJV

When they are sick, lying upon their bed of suffering, God will restore them. He will raise them up again and restore them back to health. So in my sickness I say to you, 'Lord, be my kind healer. Heal my body and soul; heal me, God! For I have confessed my sins to you.'

- Psalms 41:3-4, TPT

Blessed be the LORD, that hath given rest unto his people Israel, according to all that he promised: there hath not failed one word of all his good promise, which he promised by the hand of Moses his servant.

- 1 Kings 8:56, KJV

My covenant will I not break, nor alter the thing that is gone out of my lips.

- Psalms 89:34, KJV

With long life will I satisfy him, and shew him my salvation.

- Psalms 91:16, KJV

You will be satisfied with a full life and with all that I do for you. For you will enjoy the fullness of my salvation!

- Psalms 91:16, TPT

Bless the LORD, O my soul: and all that is within me, bless his holy name. Bless the LORD, O my soul, and forget not all his benefits: Who forgiveth all thine iniquities; who healeth all thy diseases; Who redeemeth thy life from destruction; who crowneth thee with lovingkindness and tender mercies; Who satisfieth thy mouth with good things; so that thy youth is renewed like the eagle's.

- Psalms 103:1-5, TPT

With my whole heart, with my whole life, and with my innermost being, I bow in wonder and love before you, the holy God! Yahweh, you are my soul's celebration. How could I ever forget the miracles of kindness you've done for me? You kissed my heart with forgiveness, in spite of all I've done. You've healed me inside and out from every disease. You've rescued me from hell and saved my life. You've crowned me with love and mercy. You satisfy my every desire with good things. You've supercharged my life so that I soar again like a flying eagle in the sky!

- Psalms 107:20, KJV

He sent his word, and healed them, and delivered them from their destructions. God spoke the words 'Be healed, 'and we were healed, delivered from death's door!"

- Psalms 107:20, TPT

I shall not die, but live, and declare the works of the LORD.

- Psalms 118:17, KJV

293

My son, attend to my words; incline thine ear unto my sayings. Let them not depart from thine eyes; keep them in the midst of thine heart. For they are life unto those that find them, and health to all their flesh.

- Proverbs 4:20-22, KJV

'I, only I, am He who wipes out your transgressions for My own sake, And I will not remember your sins. Remind Me [of your merits with a thorough report], let us plead and argue our case together; State your position, that you may be proved right.'

Isaiah 43:25-26, AMP

Surely he hath borne our (griefs) - (Heb. means: Sickness) and carried our (sorrows:) - (Heb. means: Pains) yet we did esteem him stricken, smitten of God, and afflicted. But he was wounded for our transgressions, he was bruised for our iniquities: the chastisement of our peace was upon him; and with his stripes we are healed.

- Isaiah 53:4-5, KJV,

Etymology Provided by the Author

Then said the LORD unto me, Thou hast well seen: for I will hasten my word to perform it.

- Jeremiah 1:12, KJV

Then the LORD said to me, 'You have seen well, for I am [actively] watching over My word to fulfill it.'

- Jeremiah 1:12, AMP

For I will restore health unto thee, and I will heal thee of thy wounds, saith the LORD; because they called thee an Outcast, saying, This is Zion, whom no man seeketh after.

- Jeremiah 30:17, KJV

'For I will restore health to you And I will heal your wounds,' says the LORD, 'Because they have called you an outcast, saying: 'This is Zion; no one seeks her and no one cares for her.'

- Jeremiah 30:17, AMP

What do ye imagine against the LORD? he will make an utter end: affliction shall not rise up the second time.

- Nahum 1:9, KJV

Whatever [plot] you [Assyrians] devise against the LORD, He will make a complete

end of it; Affliction [of God's people by the hand of Assyria] will not occur twice.

- Nahum 1:9, AMP

... so that He fulfilled what was spoken by the prophet Isaiah: 'HE HIMSELF TOOK

OUR INFIRMITIES [upon Himself] AND CARRIED AWAY OUR DISEASES.'

- Matthew 8:17, AMP
- Emphasis made by author

I assure you and most solemnly say to you, whatever you bind [forbid, declare to be improper and unlawful] on earth shall have [already] been bound in heaven, and whatever you loose [permit, declare lawful] on earth shall have [already] been loosed in heaven. 'Again I say to you, that if two believers on earth agree [that is, are of one mind, in harmony] about anything that they ask [within the will of God], it will be done for them by My Father in heaven.'

- Matthew 18:18-19, AMP

Yet I totally trust you to rescue me one more time, so that I can see once again how good you are while I'm still alive! Here's what I've learned through it all: Don't give up; don't be impatient; be entwined as one with the Lord. Be brave and courageous, and never lose hope. Yes, keep on waiting—for he will never disappoint you!

\- Psalms 27:13-14, TPT

Jesus replied, 'Listen to the truth. If you have no doubt of God's power and speak out of faith's fullness, you can be the ones who speak to a tree and it will wither away. Even more than that, you could say to this mountain, 'Be lifted up and be thrown into the sea' and it will be done. Everything you pray for with the fullness of faith you will receive!'

\- Matthew 21:21-22, TPT

Jesus replied, 'Let the faith of God be in you! Listen to the truth I speak to you: If someone says to this mountain with great faith and having no doubt, 'Mountain, be lifted up and thrown into the midst of the sea,' and believes that what he says will happen, it will be done. This is the reason I urge you to boldly believe for whatever you ask for in prayer—be convinced that you have received it and it will be yours.'

- Mark 11:22-24, TPT

And these miracle signs will accompany those who believe: They will drive out demons in the power of my name. They will speak in tongues. They will be supernaturally protected from snakes and from drinking anything poisonous. And they will lay hands on the sick and heal them.

- Mark 16:17-18, TPT

Now you understand that I have imparted to you all my authority to trample over his kingdom. You will trample upon every demon before you and overcome every power Sutan possesses. Absolutely nothing will be able to harm you as you walk in this authority.

- Luke 10:19, TPT

Yes, God raised Jesus to life! And since God's Spirit of Resurrection lives in you, he will also raise your dying body to life by the same Spirit that breathes life into you!

- Romans 8:11, TPT

For all of God's promises find their "yes" of fulfillment in him. And as his "yes" and our "amen" ascend to God, we bring him glory!

- 2 Corinthians 1:20, TPT

We can demolish every deceptive fantasy that opposes God and break through every arrogant attitude that is raised up in defiance of the true knowledge of God. We capture, like prisoners of war, every thought and insist that it bow in obedience to the Anointed One.

- 2 Corinthians 10:5, TPT

Yet, Christ paid the full price to set us free from the curse of the law. He absorbed it completely as he became a curse in our place. For it is written: 'Everyone who is hung upon a tree is doubly cursed.'

- Galatians 3:13, TPT

God will continually revitalize you, implanting within you the passion to do what pleases him.

- Philippians 2:13, TPT

For God will never give you the spirit of fear, but the Holy Spirit who gives you mighty power, love, and self-control.

- 2 Timothy 1:7, TPT

So now wrap your heart tightly around the hope that lives within us, knowing that God always keeps his promises!

- Hebrews 10:23, TPT

So then, surrender to God. Stand up to the devil and resist him and he will turn and run away from you. Move your heart closer and closer to God, and he will come even closer to you. But make sure you cleanse your life, you sinners, and keep your heart pure and stop doubting.

- James (Jacob) 4:7-8, TPT

1. Surrender

2. Resist

3. Move

4. Stop doubting

He himself carried our sins in his body on the cross so that we would be dead to sin and live for righteousness. Our instant healing flowed from his wounding.

- 1 Peter 2:24, TPT

Since we have this confidence, we can also have great boldness before him, for if we ask anything agreeable to his will, he will hear us. And if we know that he hears us in whatever we ask, we also know that we have obtained the requests we ask of him.

- 1 John 5:14-15, TPT

Beloved friend, I pray that you are prospering in every way and that you continually enjoy good health, just as your soul is prospering.

- 3 John 1:2, TPT

They conquered him completely through the blood of the Lamb and the powerful word of his testimony. They triumphed because they did not love and cling to their own lives, even when faced with death.

- Revelation 12:11, TPT

About the Author

Alissa Holt is a worldwide traveler and speaker, debut author, worship leader and songwriter. She is widely known because of her social media presence, and coaches countless women around the nation through her mentorship program called "The Crew". She calls her girls home, with two beautiful souls who are constantly teaching her how to live her best life. Those who love her best help support her Gilmore Girls-level coffee habit as well as her addiction to tacos and spicy salsa. Very rarely is she seen without a worn and weathered journal or Bible in hand, but her very best hobby is doing life with people hand in hand.

Connect with her on a daily basis, follow her story, see pictures and videos, join *The Crew*, and keep up with her travel schedule:

www.alissaholt.com

https://www.facebook.com/thealissahol t/

https://www.instagram.com/thealissaholt/

https://www.tiktok.com/@thealissaholt

YouTube: @thealissaholt

Made in the USA
Columbia, SC
19 November 2024

46972207R00167